THE MORAL ARGUMENT FOR CHRISTIAN THEISM

THE MORAL ARGUMENT
FOR CHRISTIAN THEISM

BY

H. P. OWEN

Reader in the Philosophy of Religion
at King's College in the University of London

London

GEORGE ALLEN & UNWIN LTD

RUSKIN HOUSE   MUSEUM STREET

PRINTED IN GREAT BRITAIN
in 10 *point Pilgrim type*
BY EAST MIDLAND PRINTING CO. LTD.
BURY ST. EDMUNDS

PREFACE

There are many arguments for God's existence. The best known are those which are called the ontological, the cosmological, the teleological and the moral. The last—the moral—argument is the subject of this book. I hope to show that morality gives us firm grounds for believing in a transcendent, personal and holy God.

However, the word 'argument' can be misleading. I do not intend to offer a proof that will coerce assent by means of formal logic; for I do not think that such a proof is possible from moral or from any other premisses. Discursive thought, operating on non-theistic evidence, can give 'reasons for' belief in God; but belief itself cannot be acquired without an act of intuition.

The first philosopher to formulate the moral argument was Kant. It has since been used by many distinguished thinkers. I need mention only John Henry Newman, Hastings Rashdall, Clement Webb, and A. E. Taylor. Of these I owe a special debt to Newman and Taylor. The former's *Grammar of Assent* and the latter's *The Faith of a Moralist* deserve to be placed among the classics of philosophy.

If I were asked why I chose to write on this (in preference to any other) argument I should give two reasons. Firstly, I do not think that the argument has recently been given the prominence it intrinsically deserves. Secondly, I also think that a fresh presentation of it may help to make Christian theism more intelligible and meaningful to believers and unbelievers equally; for every reflecting person must be concerned to discover the metaphysical foundations of his moral life.

The plan of the book is as follows. In chapter one I shall discuss the nature of morality (in so far as this is relevant to my theme); in chapter two I shall describe the main elements in the relation between morality and faith; in chapters three, four, and five I shall consider the moral argument through the concepts of

7

Duty, Goodness, and Beatitude; finally, in chapter six, I shall try to show how the argument is fulfilled in Christian revelation.

I wish to thank Professor H. D. Lewis and Professor E. L. Mascall for their kind interest, advice, and encouragement, Miss A. M. Wyatt for typing my (often untidy) manuscript so efficiently, and my publishers for their friendliness.

CONTENTS

Chapter 1

THE NATURE OF MORALITY

'Morality' is derived from the Latin *mos*, and 'ethics' from the Greek ἦθος. Both the Latin and the Greek words can mean 'custom', 'habit', or 'behaviour'. If we follow etymology we shall say that theories of morality, or ethics, have as their subject-matter the ways in which people behave. They describe modes of human conduct.

Yet, as usual, etymology is not itself sufficient. Morality indicates, not simply how people behave, but how they ought to behave. The word 'ought' is crucial. The moralist deals with conduct in so far as it is 'good' or 'bad', 'right' or 'wrong'. A theory of morals is (among other things) an attempt to elucidate the meaning of these adjectives.

Because morality has as its *differentiae* the good and the bad, the right and the wrong, the study of moral conduct is distinct from psychology. The psychologist describes human actions, but he does not evaluate them. Values may enter into his description, but he does not analyse them *per se*. Their intrinsic nature is not, and cannot be, his concern.[1]

The words 'behaviour' and 'conduct' are still too vague as definitions of the objects to which moral judgments apply. 'Right' and 'wrong', 'good' and 'bad', can qualify dispositions,

---

[1] This is admitted by most psychologists. Thus J. C. Flugel, in his *Man, Morals and Society* (London 1962), writes that psychology, being descriptive not normative, 'has no concern with values as such' (p. 16). Yet he inconsistently affirms on p. 21 that 'the psychological is tending *to replace* the moral point of view', and on p. 23 that 'values are *determined* by our biological nature and our innate psychological equipment' (italics mine). Psychology can certainly be relevant to particular moral judgments and decisions; but it cannot (so long as it remains a purely empirical science) determine either the meaning or the validity of ethical concepts.

motives, intentions, actions and consequences. Every moral situation has these five constituents. Moreover each constituent needs to be considered separately.

This chapter has a limited aim: to inquire into the *status* of moral terms. I wish to maintain firstly that they are irreducible, unique; and secondly that they are capable of being given a fully objective reference. Unless these two theses can be maintained it is impossible to take morality as a ground for belief in God—or indeed to believe in God at all.

The first point to be established is one that I have already implied in my provisional distinction between ethics and psychology. Morality is unique. It cannot be reduced to non-moral terms. Several attempts at reduction have been made. It has been said that 'good' and 'right' *mean* (for example), 'the pleasant', 'the more evolved', 'the completely satisfying', 'the realization of the self'. All these forms of reductionism were grouped together under the one label 'The Naturalistic Fallacy' by G. E. Moore in his *Principia Ethica* which was first published in 1903. While I do not like the word 'naturalistic', and while I find Moore's own view of goodness as an indefinable quality unacceptable, the fallacy remains one under any other name. The name that I choose is 'reductionism'.

The reductionist fails to observe two distinctions that are central to the moral consciousness.

Firstly, the distinction between description and evaluation. We have already seen that this distinction separates ethics from psychology. A psychologist could describe a course of conduct through all the supposed substitutes for 'right' and 'good' that I have mentioned. Thus a Freudian could explain an act as the 'satisfaction' of the 'Id' according to the 'pleasure-pain' principle. But this does not in itself tell us whether the act is good or bad. If the act is simply the gratification of sensual impulses it is only too likely to be wrong.

Secondly, the distinction between 'ought' and 'is'. The reductionist attempts to derive the former from the latter. But this cannot be done if the latter is defined in non-moral terms. After we have fully explained the non-moral characteristics of an act we can still ask whether it *ought* to have been performed. Equally, after we have reviewed all the non-moral ingredients in a situation demanding choice we still have to ask how we *ought* to choose.

Reductionism is also exposed to more specific objections. I shall briefly consider a few of these. I shall first examine the equation of 'the good' with 'the pleasant'. Its absurdity was trenchantly exposed by Moore as follows:—

'There is no meaning in saying that pleasure is good, unless good is something different from pleasure. It is absolutely useless, so far as Ethics is concerned, to prove, as Mr. Spencer tries to do, that increase of pleasure coincides with increase of life, unless good *means* something different from either life or pleasure. He might as well try to prove that an orange is yellow by showing that it always is wrapped up in paper.'

Furthermore, those who identify 'good' with 'pleasure' frequently distinguish between different kinds of pleasure. Thus J. S. Mill was forced to affirm that some pleasures are superior on the score of their intrinsic quality or worth. But one cannot hold some pleasures to be 'better' than others without an antecedent idea of 'the good life'—that is, without interpreting 'pleasure' through 'goodness', not 'goodness' through 'pleasure'.

Again, it is much harder to reduce the concept of obligation than it is to reduce other moral concepts to hedonistic terms. There may be some initial plausibility in equating 'right' and 'good' with 'pleasant'; but it is utterly unplausible to equate 'obligation' with 'pleasure'. Even if I were to identify the rightness of a proposed action with the amount of pleasure it is likely to produce I should still have to decide whether I *ought* to perform the action.

Purely ethical hedonism of the kind that I have been considering has frequently been combined with psychological hedonism— with the view that human nature is so constituted that it *must* seek the acquisition of pleasure and the avoidance of pain. This view is open to two objections.

Firstly, it renders praise and blame inapplicable in precisely those cases where we consider them to be most relevant. There would be no point in blaming a person for performing an action which he was unable to resist. We do not censure a 'brain-machine' if it fails to achieve results for which it was not 'programmed'. Blame always, and praise often, presuppose the possibility of a free choice between the performance of duty and the pursuit of pleasure.

Secondly, introspection proves the determinist's theory to be false. We may sometimes mistake our motives and we may sometimes act from mixed ones. But we do not always do so. There are cases in which we can be sure, after the most rigorous self-analysis, that we acted out of duty in defiance of a pleasure-seeking impulse. No other hypothesis will fit the facts.

In order to meet the second of these objections psychological hedonists offer a refined, and peculiarly insidious, version of their doctrine. Even when we act out of duty, they say, we still act with a view to pleasure—the pleasure of a good conscience. To this the following answers can be given.

(a) No one could have the pleasure of a good conscience unless he first recognized obligation. In speaking of the pleasure, or satisfaction, that 'accompanies' the performance of duty the hedonist admits that the duty is primary and the pleasure secondary. I mean the words 'primary' and 'secondary' to be taken in both a logical and a chronological sense. Duty is logically prior in so far it determines both the existence and the quality of the pleasure. It is chronologically prior according to the irreversible sequence of cause and effect.

(b) It is self-contradictory to assert that one performs a duty in order to obtain pleasure. Duty, as Kant said, is essentially categorical. It cannot be conditioned by any non-moral factors whatsoever. Even to act with a view to the pleasure it entailed would be to act under a non-moral and hypothetical instead of the moral and categorical imperative.[2]

(c) The Christian has special reasons for rejecting this sophisticated brand of hedonism. He is as apt to have a bad conscience as to have a good one. Even when he has done his duty as best he can he is aware that he is an 'unprofitable servant' who

---

[2] I do not mean that an act is non-moral solely because it produces pleasure in the agent. On the contrary, the more virtuous a person is the more the pleasure will be present. Even Kant, according to Paton, 'insists that the moral life brings with it its own peculiar satisfaction or contentment' (*The Categorical Imperative* p. 57). At the same time Kant would say that the good will is one that acts for the sake of duty, not any satisfaction (in the sense of pleasure).

depends on God for the completion of his good works as much as for the expiation of his evil ones.

However, there is one all-important distinction still to be made. I have been attacking the theory that reduces moral terms to assessment in terms of pleasure. According to this theory the good *means* the pleasant, so that the relation between 'X is good' and 'X is pleasant or pleasurable' is analytic. This theory must good *means* the pleasant, so that the relation between 'X is good' ness cannot be reduced to pleasure, or the motive for duty to a pleasure-seeking impulse, pleasure or happiness will be the outcome of a moral life. There may well be a synthetic connection between goodness and pleasure, even though the pleasure (or joy) may not be completely attainable until the life to come.

I shall comment briefly on one other attempt at reductionism: Evolutionary Ethics. I choose this for several reasons. It is in itself especially interesting; it is still advocated today by Julian Huxley and C. H. Waddington; finally, its refutation (as we shall see) has an immediate bearing on the theistic argument from design.

The phrase 'evolutionary ethics' indicates any attempt to derive the meaning and validity of moral concepts from the course of evolution. Moore's phrase was Evolutionistic Naturalism under which he includes those doctrines 'which maintain that the course of evolution, while it shows us the direction in which we *are* developing, thereby and for that reason shows us the direction in which we *ought* to develop'. He then shows (with reference to Spencer) that Natural Selection cannot itself provide any ethical criteria; for it 'will explain, equally well, how by an alteration in the environment (the gradual cooling of the earth, for example) quite a different species from man, a species which we think infinitely lower, might survive us'. The conclusion Moore draws is irresistible. 'The survival of the fittest does *not* mean, as one might suppose, the survival of what is fittest to fulfil a good purpose—best adapted to a good end: at the last, it means merely the survival of the fittest to survive.'

In fact morality can be derived from evolution only if evolution is read in the light of preconceived moral terms. Morality is first equated with what is 'more evolved' or 'what is determined by evolutionary direction'; but what is more evolved—

the direction which the evolutionary process takes—turns out to be what is in accordance with those moral standards that we independently possess. The evolutionist's argument is circular.

This circularity is revealed with especial clarity in a recent book by Julian Huxley.[3] Having stated that 'evolutionary direction' requires us to cultivate the fulfilment of human potentialities he immediately adds these crucial words. 'Of course, not all fulfilment or all enjoyment is good or right, any more than all biological improvement is progressive. It is the business of moral systems to make such evaluations' (p. 150). On Huxley's own admission the evolutionary process does not provide us with moral criteria. Rather, these criteria tell us the direction which the process ought to take.

A more subtle (though also more confusing) version of the doctrine has recently been propounded by C. H. Waddington.[4] While Waddington rejects a naturalistic reduction of ethical to non-ethical terms,[5] and while he charges Julian Huxley's argument with circularity,[6] he still believes that it is possible to judge ethical beliefs 'according to their efficacy in furthering general evolutionary direction'.[7] Yet he utterly fails to justify the beliefs he outlines in the last two chapters by an appeal to the mechanism of 'socio-genetic' transmission that he has previously described. As an example here is his account of the reasons why we should encourage the 'co-existence' of Capitalism and Communism.

'The complete obliteration of either would gravely impoverish what one might call the "Idea Pool" of the human species: the store of socially transmittable variations which are available as the raw material for future evolution. When one is dealing with a relatively localized cultural development with a narrow range of ideas, such as Nazism was, the elimination of the whole thing may be advantageous if that rids man of a number of ideas

---

[3] *Evolution in Action.* (London 1963). The many fallacies in Huxley's reasoning have been incisively exposed by Stephen Toulmin in an essay in *Metaphysical Beliefs* (London 1957). Toulmin shows how Huxley flatly contradicts his grandfather, T. H. Huxley, who held that our ethical judgments, so far from being justified by biological evolution, reverse it by substituting the elimination of the weak with compassion for them.
[4] *The Ethical Animal* (London 1960).   [5] pp. 46 and 52.
[6] pp. 58-9.   [7] p. 7.

which impede anagenesis, at the expense of only a few potentially valuable ones.'[8]

The crux is contained in the word 'valuable'. If we say that
Capitalism and Communism (unlike Nazism) deserve to survive
because of their superior 'value', and if we mean *moral* value,
we are plainly using a criterion to which biology is entirely
irrelevant; so that Waddington's reasoning is no less circular than
that of Huxley. 'Value' interprets 'anagenesis'; but 'anagenesis'
cannot interpret 'value'.

I come now to the second problem raised by the inquiry into
the status of moral terms. It is not enough to say that they are
irreducible. One must also say that they are 'objective'.

The notion of 'objectivity' in ethics has been much discussed
in recent literature. But in ethics, as in other spheres, the words
'objective' and 'subjective' become the cause of serious confusion unless they are carefully defined. I wish to distinguish
between three ethical meanings they can bear.

(1) When we speak of values possessing 'objectivity' we can
mean that they exist in an absolute form outside the world of
sense-experience. 'Objective' in this sense signifies 'independent'.
Values exist (or subsist) independently of their instances in a
purely spiritual realm. Plato thought of them as existing 'on their
own', without any further ground. The Christian interprets them
as attributes of God.

(2) Sometimes we use the word 'objective' in the sense of
'universal'. An objective standard, ideal, or norm is one which
everyone does, or ought to, recognize. So it could be held that
kindness and loyalty are 'objective' in the sense of being ideals
of conduct at which all persons ought to aim. This view of ethical
objectivity implies that all men have (potentially if not actually)
a common moral nature.

Those who use objective in this sense usually feel compelled
to distinguish between 'objective' and 'subjective' rightness. An
act is right 'objectively' if it conforms to objective norms. But
an act is right 'subjectively' if it is performed according to the
dictates of the agent's conscience. It follows that an act pre-
scribed by an unenlightened, though sincere, conscience would
(unless the lack of enlightenment was culpable) be right in a

[8] pp. 210-11.

subjective though not an objective sense.[9]

(3) When we apply a moral attribute we may do so either objectively or subjectively. If we do so objectively we mean that the attribute inheres objectively in the person, act, or state of affairs to which it is applied. 'Goodness' or 'rightness' belongs to X as objectively as X's physical properties belong to it. This view implies that moral judgments have the following characteristics:—

(a) They are descriptive. When we call X good we are describing it as it is 'in itself' quite as much as if we were to call it round or square. We are adding a new piece of information concerning it.

(b) They are capable of being true or false. Indeed they *must* be either true or false. It either is or is not the case that X is good. It is as true or false to say 'X is good' as it is to say 'the grass is wet'.

(c) They must ultimately rest on 'intuition'. If goodness actually inheres as a 'non-natural' quality in objects it is apprehended by an intellectual act analogous to our perception of their physical qualities.

On the other hand to call moral terms 'subjective' is to locate their *designata* in an activity of the subject-user. On this view, when I call X 'good' I am merely recording my own attitude. I am approving, praising, or commending X. But I am in no way affirming that it possesses goodness 'in itself'. Since the sentence 'X is good' does not refer to any property of X it cannot be true or false—except in the sense that the speaker may be either honest or dishonest in his statement of approval.

This subjectivist account of moral judgments is held in varying forms by many contemporary philosophers—for example Ayer, Stevenson, Nowell-Smith and Hare. This element in modern empiricism, like every other, can be traced back to Hume.

In the rest of this chapter I shall try to show (a) that both 'goodness' and 'rightness' are objective in the second and third

[9] Hence, when I said in the preceding paragraph that all men 'ought' to aim at objective ideals I meant 'ought' in the moral sense to apply only in those cases where the objectivity of the ideal is recognized. One cannot have a duty to pursue ideals of which one is unaware. But in the *teleological* sense of 'ought' all men without exception ought to accept these ideals if in fact they are ideals for human nature as such.

of these senses, and (b) that a further consideration of rightness will reveal that moral 'claims' are objective in the first sense also. Perhaps my arguments will not convince the subjectivist. Ultimately every ethical system rests on a few truths that are taken to be self-evident.

So far as goodness is concerned the crucial sense of 'objectivity' is the third. When we call a person 'good' do we mean that goodness actually inheres in him as a characteristic of his nature or a quality of his being? (I choose the example of a person, not a thing, for a reason that will become apparent shortly). The subjectivist holds that we do not mean this. We intend—or when enlightened by philosophical analysis we come to see that we intend—only to express our approval of the person.

However, it is necessary to distinguish between subjectivism in its earlier and crude form (as represented by Ayer in his *Language, Truth and Logic*) and its later, more sophisticated, form (as represented by Nowell-Smith in his *Ethics*). According to the crude form there is *no* objective basis for moral terms; they are *wholly* reducible to subjective feelings. According to the more sophisticated form objective criteria for the use of 'good' exist; but 'good' itself expresses simply the approval of the user.

The crude form is exposed to an unanswerable objection. If moral judgments are merely expressions (or descriptions) of approval it is impossible to understand how they can become the cause of rational disagreement. If I like tea and my friend likes coffee I do not attempt to convert him. But if I hear someone commending the conduct of a rogue I consider his opinion to be dangerously wrong. Clearly I am justified in condemning someone else's moral judgment only if I can give reasons for my condemnation. It is the absence of any reasons for my preference for tea which makes it absurd for me to challenge my friend's preference for coffee. In other words, if my moral preferences are to be rational they must be based on criteria of an objective kind.

The emotivism of Ayer has consequently been modified in order to admit the existence of such criteria. This is how Nowell-Smith puts it : —

'It is improper to use "good", at least as an impersonal formula, to express or defend a preference unless the preference is a considered one, based on reasons, and not unusual. And to say that the preference is "based on reasons" is to say that the speaker applied criteria or standards. It is not necessary that he should have done this deliberately; he may have done it automatically; but he must be able to defend his choice by an appeal to the standards which justify it.'[10]

Yet this acknowledgement of objective criteria does not prevent Nowell-Smith from endorsing the essential element in subjectivism; for he still maintains that the word 'good' indicates no more than an attitude of approval.[11] Thus while I call X good *because* he is (for example) kind and courageous, and while kindness and courage are properties of his character, 'good' itself refers to my 'pro-attitude'.[12]

However, even in this later form subjectivism contradicts experience. Let us suppose I have a friend whom I admire. He is honest and kind in all his dealings with me. He is (as I should put it) always 'good to' me. Can I suppose that 'good' in this context merely refers to my 'pro-attitude'? On the contrary, the more I know of him the more I feel his goodness as an objective fact that confronts me and compels my admiration. Admittedly this appeal to experience does not constitute an argument; but such an appeal is ultimately inevitable.

Goodness, I submit, is neither a simple property distinct from

---

[10] *Ethics* (London 1961, p. 170).

[11] He consistently abides by his earlier statement that 'to say that something is good is not to make a statement about it or to describe it, but to express a desire for or an attitude towards it, to express approval of it, to grade it, to praise it, to commend it, and so on' (op. cit. p. 95).

[12] A position similar to that of Nowell-Smith is held by R. M. Hare. In his recent *Freedom and Reason* (Oxford, 1963, pp. 22-24) Hare admits that there are objective criteria for the use of 'good'; but 'good' itself does not have any objective reference; it merely *prescribes* for imitation the forms of conduct that it specifies. A full and judicious account of the emotivists and their successors is given by Brand Blanshard (*Reason and Goodness*, London 1961, pp. 194-265). Blanshard shows that while such philosophers as Hare, Toulmin, and Urmson have retreated from the earlier emotivism of Carnap, Ayer, and Stevenson, by admitting the existence of objective grounds for the use of 'good' 'none of them has conceded that a judgment of good is a judgment in a straightforward sense at all' (p. 265).

the qualities that act as its criteria; nor does it refer merely to a pro-attitude that these qualities evoke; it exists in and through the latter which are its modes of operation. When I call someone's honesty and kindness his 'good points' I mean that they are dispositions and activities in which his goodness is revealed.[13]

Advocates of subjectivism often fail to distinguish between two spheres to which moral judgments can apply: states of affairs and persons. The distinction is vitally important both in itself and in relation to religious faith.

In seeking to establish the objectivity of goodness I have chosen personal examples. Here it seems to me that objectivism is self-evidently true. When we are confronted with a good or, still more, holy person we are convinced that worth inheres in his character and will. But when goodness is attributed to a state of affairs or situation the subjectivist's analysis is convincing. Here the only plausible thing to say is that we are expressing our approval. We could substitute 'desirable' for 'good' without any loss of meaning.

Let us suppose that we see two groups of children. The first group is well-treated, healthy, and contented. The second group is ill-treated, starved, and miserable. We should have no hesitation in calling the situation of the first group good and the situation of the second group evil. But it is hard to see how good and evil could inhere as non-empirical properties in the facts described. Here it is natural to interpret moral terms as indications of our attitudes. We commend the first situation as strongly as we deplore the second.

However, the subjective status of 'good' in sentences referring to situations derives its meaning from its objective status when it is applied to human wills. A good situation is one which a good person would desire or commend. It is through this primary, though indirect, reference to a good or evil will that we judge a situation to be good or evil in a secondary and subjective

---

[13] I should therefore agree with H. W. B. Joseph that goodness, so far from being a simple quality like yellow (as Moore believed), is a self-diversifying unity that constitutes a 'form' of being (*Some Problems in Ethics*, Oxford 1931, pp. 75-87). But I doubt whether Joseph saw that we cannot *identify* goodness with being in the case of any *man*; for it is only in God that essence and existence are identical.

sense.[14]

We must observe the same distinction in speaking of 'intrinsic' goodness. When we say that X is 'intrinsically' good we may be using 'good' in either a subjective or an objective sense. In the first sense X is desirable 'in itself', while in the second sense X possesses goodness as a property. Many things are morally desirable 'in themselves' (that is, quite apart from further ends to which they may be means); but it is only in a will that moral goodness can inhere.

The incapacity of subjectivism to account for human goodness is further shown by the following considerations.

(1) It is possible to attribute goodness to a person without experiencing a pro-attitude. On the one hand envy or resentment may render us incapable of feeling the approval that we know is due. On the other hand a person's goodness may be of so high an order that the very idea of approval seems inappropriate. Could we say that St Peter 'approved' of Jesus when he said 'Depart from me; for I am a sinful man, O Lord'?[15]

(2) The unnaturalness of subjectivism becomes especially plain when we consider that there must be many meritorious actions which have never been observed. But it is absurd to say that an act of heroism performed in secret now cannot be 'good' until it is praised by someone later. It is equally absurd to say that an act of cruelty is not evil until it is discovered and condemned.

(3) Even a modified subjectivism fails to account for moral disagreement. Admittedly Nowell-Smith provides criteria by which 'pro-' and 'con-' attitudes can be justified. But since these criteria do not refer to goodness as an objective (that is, intrinsic) property they cannot act as objective (that is, absolute and uni-

---

[14] Hence I should agree wholeheartedly with W. R. Sorley when he wrote: 'Goodness—when we distinguish it from beauty and truth—does not belong to material things, but to persons only' (*Moral Values and the Idea of God*, Cambridge 1918, p. 120). 'Pain' is a test-case. I should certainly hold that pain is objectively evil in a non-moral (teleological) sense in so far as it is a privation of the body's good. But it seems to me meaningless to say that it is in itself *morally* evil. Evil in the moral sense can surely be attributed (as an objective property) only to the character and will of someone who either inflicts or permits the infliction of pain out of negligence or cruelty.

[15] Lk. 5. 8.

The Nature of Morality

versal) norms. There are still no rational grounds for differing from a person who affirms that he has chosen other criteria for his moral attitudes.

Yet the moral consciousness testifies to standards, principles or norms in the light of which we judge a person good or evil. In dealing with war-criminals the Nuremberg tribunal did not say: 'You have your criteria which allows you to approve the extermination of the Jewish race; we have different ones which compel us to condemn it; therefore we are going to execute you.' Rather it said (or implied): 'Genocide is absolutely evil; those who practise it are evil; therefore they deserve to die.'

The degree to which subjectivism misrepresents experience is shown by Russell's attempt to explain why he prefers Buddhist to Nietzschean ethics.

'For my part, I agree with Buddha as I have imagined him. But I do not know how to prove that he is right by any arguments such as can be used in a mathematical or a scientific question. I dislike Nietzsche because he likes the contemplation of pain, because he erects conceit into duty, because the men whom he most admires are conquerors, whose glory is cleverness in causing men to die. But I think the ultimate argument against his philosophy, as against any unpleasant but internally self-consistent ethic, lies not in an appeal to facts, but in an appeal to the emotions. Nietzsche despises universal love; I feel it the motive power to all that I desire as regards the world. His followers have had their innings, but we may hope that it is coming rapidly to an end'.[16]

Russell, like Nowell-Smith, has objective criteria for his use of 'good' and 'evil'. The Buddha's system is good because it is based on 'universal love'; Nietzsche's system is bad because he enjoys the thought of suffering. Yet good and evil represent our attitudes; they stand for emotions, not for facts. Hence Russell is reduced to saying that the Nietzschean system is 'unpleasant'. If he is to avoid naturalism he must mean *morally* unpleasant. But even when so qualified the adjective cannot do justice to our attitude; for the latter consists in the *judgment* 'this is wrong'. Furthermore unless the actions that displease us are intrinsically

[16] *History of Western Philosophy* (London 1957, p. 800).

23

wrong we have no right to dissuade (much less restrain) people from performing them. The fact that Russell desires universal love may be biographically interesting; but it is ethically un-informative; for it does not help us to decide which desires we *ought* to cultivate.

I am well aware that the belief in objective norms raises many problems. Two are especially pressing. Firstly, since different social groups acknowledge different moral norms how do we know which norms are in fact objective? Secondly, can we call a person bad if he lives conscientiously by mistaken norms?

The only answer to the first question is that we 'know' by intuition. The final principles of morality, like those of meta-physics, are self-authenticating or self-evident. Even the sub-jectivist must employ the power of intuition that he so frequently maligns; for even he is sure that his criteria are the ones that *merit* a pro-attitude. Anyone who chooses any moral code in preference to another must be convinced that his criteria are the best; and ultimately the judgment 'this is the best' is based on intuition.

Obviously we may think that we intuit goodness when in fact we are mistaken. Either we have chosen the wrong norms or we have failed to discern correctly their embodiment in human character. But morality is not the only sphere in which we make mistakes. Scientists have often taken something to be true which experiment has subsequently demonstrated to be false.

If we identify certitude in the moral sphere with the certainty attainable in mathematics—if we take non-contradictability as the test of moral truth—we shall always be unsure that our convictions are correct; but equally on this test we could never believe in the existence of either material objects or other human selves. To this extent an act of *synteresis* is closer to an act of sense-perception than it is to formal reasoning.[17]

In answer to the second question I should say that it is neces-sary to make two distinctions. The first is between perverted and defective norms. The second is between the conscientiousness with which a person embodies norms and the character that this embodiment entails.

---

[17] In fact moral progress does not consist in substituting wholly true norms for wholly false ones. Rather it consists in criticizing, refining, and re-ordering norms that are already partly true.

The first distinction may be illustrated thus. A Nazi who deliberately prefers violence to compassion or a Communist who systematically puts the advantage of his party above the claim of truth is living by perverted norms. But Aristotle's picture of the 'magnanimous man', while defective from an altruistic standpoint, contains at least some of the virtues which contribute to perfection.

The second distinction corresponds to the one I have already made between subjective and objective rightness. We can judge a person good with reference either to norms *per se* or to his conscientiousness in observing them. A person who lives by perverted norms cannot be good however 'conscientious' he may be. But we distinguish between character and conscientiousness in those who live by deficient norms. Thus while we could say that the character (and in this sense the goodness) of St Francis is of an intrinsically higher order than the character of Socrates because St Francis had access to intrinsically higher norms we should not, I take it, wish to qualify our attribution of goodness to Socrates on the score of his disinterested devotion to the norms at his disposal.

The Christian, however, has no excuse for applying this distinction to himself or even (in misdirected tolerance) to his fellow-Christians; for he believes that the ideal for human life is finally given in the New Testament. If someone says that yet a higher ideal may emerge he cannot be refuted by either deductive or inductive logic; but the absence of logical refutation is inevitable.[18]

I turn now to consider the concept of 'rightness'. This is related to the concepts of 'obligation', 'duty', 'law', and 'claims'. A right action is one that the agent feels 'obliged' to perform from a sense of 'duty' towards the moral 'law' or moral 'claims'. It seems to me plain that 'right', like 'good', is objective in my second and third senses.

[18] Of course the finality of moral norms is confirmed if they are also objective in the first sense that I gave—if they are grounded in 'ultimate reality' (e.g. Plato's Forms or the Christian God). Whether such confirmation is forthcoming is a question that I shall discuss later. Meanwhile I merely wish to state (as I shall have cause to re-state in the next chapter) that the finality of moral norms can be (and must be) accepted on moral grounds alone.

'Rightness' can be objective in the second sense. It can indicate a standard, principle, or norm. When we say that truth-telling and promise-keeping are right we mean that they are right for every rational person irrespective of his feelings and desires. Admittedly there is no way of proving their objective rightness. But those who deny it must face the same criticisms that I brought against those who deny the objectivity of 'good'.

Yet is rightness also objective in the third sense? Does it inhere in human acts? This is a difficult question, and I can only outline an answer to it.

If 'act' is equated with outward, observable, behaviour I cannot see how any act is right 'in itself'. The rightness surely lies in a right intention—that is, an intention to obey the moral law. Unless the will is good the action, while appearing to be right, is not really so. Thus a person who subscribed to a relief-fund solely to enhance his reputation would not be acting rightly. All we can say is that his action *would* have been right if it had been governed by the universal law of charity.

I now wish to maintain that the concept of right implies objectivity in my first sense also. The norms of rightness possess an independent mode of being. I know that this thesis will seem strange to many readers. But it is clearly necessitated by the nature of 'obligation', 'law', and 'claims'.

Let us first consider claims. When we call an action right we mean that it is appropriate. Yet we do not mean appropriate in any pragmatic or prudential sense. We mean that it is required by a moral claim. Now a claim is something that confronts us. But how can it confront us unless it has real existence?

If we substitute 'law' for 'claims' we reach the same conclusion. The moral 'law' comprises the principles or norms that make an action right or wrong. Yet it is also a command—a 'categorical imperative' requiring unconditional obedience. But how can the law command unless it exists either 'in itself' or in the will of a divine Lawgiver?

Finally we can say that the moral law, or order of claims, is obligatory. The very word 'obligation' carries an objective reference. It stands for that which, coming from without, constrains and binds us. Through their obligatory character claims exert a pressure that is as real as any which is exerted by objects in the material world. Therefore they must possess their own distinctive mode of being.

If the empiricist objects that I am 'reifying' claims unnecessarily I can only reply that the 'reification' is demanded by the analytical procedure that he himself adopts. If we confine ourselves to impersonal statements (such as 'it is a duty' or 'it is right') we can perhaps evade their ontological implications. But we cannot do so if we speak personally by saying 'I must' or 'I am bound'. In moments of temptation we are aware of two orders competing for our assent: the order of our desires with their insistent clamour, and the order of claims with their unconditional demands.[19]

The only way of evading the ontological objectivity of claims without falling into the naturalistic fallacy is to locate them either in the self as the agent of moral action or in the self as the object of it.

According to the first of these alternatives the imperative of the moral law is an act of self-legislation. But while we *enact* the law we do not *give* it. On the contrary we find it already *given*. If we try to circumvent this obvious fact by saying that our 'higher' (legislating) self is a mode or self-expression of a moral Absolute we are locating the law (and its authority) in the Absolute, not in ourselves.

According to the second alternative claims are identical with the self as the *object* of moral actions. This view can be supported by two arguments.

Firstly, it is true that claims inhere in human personality. The whole of our public and private lives is a network of reciprocal rights and claims. A child exerts a claim on his parents' care; and the parents, as they grow old, have a right to expect that this care will be returned. On a larger, less personal, scale the state and its citizens possess both claims and rights in relation to each other.

Secondly, even abstract claims—actions and attitudes that are obligatory *per se*—are usually found in a personal setting. Thus truth-telling means telling the truth to a particular person.

---

[19] Those logical analysts who, taking their cue from Wittgenstein, stress the importance of studying language in its living contexts have still to learn that the full bearing of moral terms cannot be understood outside the context of existential choice.

Similarly promise-keeping means keeping our promise to the person to whom we gave it. The second example is especially cogent. A promise or a promiser without a promisee is self-contradictory.

However, duties transcend any person to whom they may be owed. This transcendence is shown by our unspoken words in moments of temptation. When tempted to neglect the fulfilment of a promise we say to ourselves: 'No, I *must* (or I am *bound*) to keep my word.' We think of the claim as something that exerts its own distinctive pressure. We need not think of the promisee at all. The only duty of which we need be aware is our debt of obedience to the moral law. Correspondingly when we have failed to keep our word we have a sense of guilt at having 'let down' both the moral order and the promisee.

Moreover, there are some moral claims which do not have any reference to other people. Thus we feel we ought to develop our talents quite apart from any duty that we owe towards (let us say) our family or the State. We are also obliged to perform further acts (for example to preserve our health) which will enable us to actualize our mental powers. Hence gluttony and sloth are 'deadly sins'.

Nevertheless, I admit that this belief in the objectivity of claims must fact two criticisms with which I shall try to deal.

1. The belief is often considered to be incompatible with the differences between moral codes. The agreement of many percipients is the most reliable criterion for the existence of material objects. But in the moral life an analogous agreement is often not forthcoming. On this I wish to make the following observations.

(a) The variations between moral codes can be, and often is, exaggerated. Even primitive peoples require fidelity to an oath, respect for the aged, and kindness towards strangers. The area of agreement is even larger among the civilized portions of mankind. The cardinal virtues of the Greeks were embodied in the moral code of medieval Christendom. Today a humanist, a Hindu and a Christian could all agree that truthfulness, courage, and compassion are among the principal virtues that they are obliged to cultivate.

(b) One must distinguish between the form and the content

of moral obligation.[20] Duties may vary; but duty itself remains the same. At some time and in some mode people of every race have glimpsed a moral order that transcends their finite selves and enforces unconditional claims. They have differed in their description of these claims; but they have been at one in affirming the absolute authority which the claims exert.

(c) In any case, even if we admit a wide variety between moral codes, and even if there are people who do not acknowledge any absolute moral law, we could still maintain that such a law exists. All we have to concede is that it requires training to perceive both the existence and the nature of the law.

This concession, so far from being a desperate expedient, is entirely reasonable. Man's understanding of his physical environment has grown from crude beginnings. So too his apprehension of his moral environment has been continuously expanded and refined. But moral progress is not uniform. We today are blind to claims that our ancestors saw clearly. We may also believe that we are blind to other claims that will appear self-evident to future generations.

2. The second criticism is based on the fact of competing claims. We are aware, as W. D. Ross has put it, that claims have only *prima facie* force. Thus we have a *prima facie* duty to tell the truth; but sometimes we are obliged to lie. How can we reconcile this conflict between claims with their objectivity? I should answer this question along the following lines.

(a) Whenever a claim is practicable it is unconditional. Thus whenever there are no countermanding claims we are unconditionally obliged to tell the truth. The fact that a morally uncontested claim is unconditional is sufficient evidence of its objectivity. Many, if not most, moral choices are of a simple kind. The choice is between a single claim (or a set of noncompeting claims) and our own self-centred inclinations.

(b) When two claims (for example, generosity and justice) cannot be enacted simultaneously we recognize that the moral order can be only partially fulfilled. In other words we are forced to admit gaps between what ought to be and what is, between value and existence. These gaps constitute a moral

[20] As H. H. Farmer has put it, 'it is the *form* of the demand as absolute and unconditional, and not so much the *content*, which is the significant thing' (*Revelation and Religion*, London 1954, p. 141).

tragedy that (so I shall argue later) cannot be overcome unless we posit a final, reconciling, act of God. If God is the source of all claims he will satisfy them in and through his creatures at his appointed time.

(c) There is always one, invariably unconditional, demand: to discharge duties as faithfully as one can. This is the one universal claim that meets us in all particular claims. We must always attempt to satisfy the latter to the best of our ability. Having done that we can do no more.

I have defended moral objectivity on purely rational grounds, for unless it is granted the moral argument for God's existence cannot even start. Unless goodness can be given an objective sense in the premiss (where it refers to finite being) it cannot have this sense in the conclusion (where it refers to the infinite being of God).

It may be said that the moral argument has a weaker basis than the other arguments in so far as it involves a special interpretation of its data. But all the arguments involve the use of categories which the radical empiricist would reject. The cosmological argument presupposes the existence of objectively necessitated causal sequences (denied by Hume). Again, the teleological argument rests on the assumption (denied by behaviourists) that mind is substantially distinct from matter. Metaphysical principles are implied by theism in all its forms.

Furthermore, much more is involved than the thesis of this book. The very idea of God is at stake. If finite worth does not objectively exist it is meaningless to speak in any form or on any grounds of its eternal Archetype.

NOTE: In a comprehensive study entitled *The Concept of Law*, H. L. A. Hart rejects as 'obscure metaphysics' the idea of 'obligation or duty as invisible objects mysteriously existing "above" or "behind" the world of ordinary, observable facts'. (pp. 81-82). But his own theory is still more obscure. On p. 84 he says that 'rules are conceived and spoken of as imposing obligations when the general demand for conformity is insistent and the social pressure brought to bear upon those who deviate or threaten to deviate is great'. He makes this statement more precise by adding that 'what is important is that the insistence of importance or *seriousness* of social pressure behind the rules is the primary factor determining whether they are thought of as giving rise to obligations'. Similarly on p. 165 he affirms that moral (as against conventional or legal) rules are distinguished by 'the serious social pressure by which they are supported'.

From these statements the reader might infer that Hart wishes to *identify* moral with social pressure. But such an identification (which would be a clear case of the naturalistic fallacy) is untenable; for, firstly, we can always ask *why* we ought to obey the dictates of society, and, secondly, we ought to resist them when they are (as they often are) corrupt. Furthermore, Hart himself admits that 'moral pressure is characteristically, though not exclusively, exerted not by threats or by appeals to fear or interest, but by reminders of the moral character of the action contemplated and of the demands of morality' (p. 175). While Hart implies that the 'reminders' are given by society (or by the agent when he reflects on the social necessity of moral norms) he also affirms that the pressure itself, being purely moral, is irreducible.

So we are back, where we started, with moral rules that impose their own distinctive obligations. But how can the moral law command—how can it exert a pressure and impose an obligation—unless it objectively exists? And how can its mode of existence be other than *super*sensible?

Chapter 2

MORALITY AND RELIGION

THIS chapter has two parts. In the first part I shall state certain basic principles which must govern any argument from morality to religion. By 'religion' I shall sometimes mean religion in general; but more often I shall mean the Christian religion in particular; for—so I shall maintain in the succeeding chapters— it is to the Christian God (the infinite and personal Creator) that morality by nature points. In the second part I shall state my attitude towards natural theology as a whole.

I suggest that five principles must govern any argument from morality to God.

1. The theist must admit that moral terms can have a self-evident meaning and validity outside the context of religious faith. He must admit this both for primary terms (such as 'right' and 'good') and for secondary ones (such as the various virtues through which goodness is expressed). The following statement by H. D. Lewis is incontrovertible:—

'There may be certain ways in which the religious person is better placed to understand the content of ethical standards—I should certainly argue that there are—but we have not to enquire into the religious antecedents of a person's actions and ascertain his religious beliefs, or lack of beliefs, before we credit him with an understanding of the nature of right and wrong and an awareness of elementary duties.[1]

It is further important to note that the unbeliever can assent

---

[1] *Morals and the New Theology* (London 1947, p. 24). See also the same writer's *Morals and Revelation* (London 1951, pp. 14-17).

to moral objectivity in the senses I have given. He can recognize the existence of moral norms, even when he fails to enact them. He can also discern their objective embodiment in a person's character and will. Finally he can see in moral claims a spiritual order that transcends his empirical self and circumstances.

The Christian theist has two especial reasons for acknowledging the plain fact that, apart from faith, values and claims are objectively self-evident.

Firstly, throughout the ages Christian thinkers have admitted that there is a 'natural' law available to unbelievers. This admission is not a 'paganization' of Christianity. It is demanded by belief in God's omnipresence through his creative Word and has a Biblical basis in St Paul's assertion that Gentiles 'show that what the law requires is written on their hearts'.[2]

Secondly, a prior grasp of moral values is necessary if we are to speak of God at all. We cannot call him loving or just unless we already know the meaning of love and justice in human life. It is true that we do not predicate any terms (not even moral ones) of God univocally. The mode of predication is always analogical. But there would be no basis for the analogy unless the terms had a self-evident finite meaning.

In particular, moral awareness is presupposed by our capacity to apprehend God in Biblical events. The culminating event —Jesus—is no exception. The authority of his teaching and the perfection of his life are among the most compelling reasons for believing him to be divine. Furthermore, it is mainly on moral grounds that we distinguish between degrees of revelation. It is by an appeal to independent moral norms that we find a clearer view of God in the Sermon on the Mount than in the imprecatory Psalms.[3]

2. Yet morality is not self-sufficient. Moral facts are not in

[2] Rom. 2.15. For further traces of natural law in the New Testament see C. H. Dodd's articles in *Theology* (1946, pp. 128-33, and 161-7).

[3] A recent book entitled *Ethics in a Christian Context* by Paul Lehmann (London 1963) shows that Christian theologians (especially those of a Barthian type) stand in constant danger of denying ethical autonomy. Lehmann calls the moral conscience 'sterile' (p. 343) and substitutes for it a 'theonomous conscience' which is 'the conscience immediately sensitive to the freedom of God to do in the always changing human situation what his humanizing aims and purposes require' (p. 358). But how can we discern, and co-operate with, God's 'humanizing aims' unless we already know, by purely moral insight, the meaning of 'humane'?

the last resort self-authenticating; they require religious justifica-
tion. The task of theism is to show how morality, when it is most
true to itself, raises questions to which the Christian concept of
God is the only answer.

There is no contradiction between acknowledging that moral
principles can be non-religiously understood and claiming that
they also require the postulation of divine existence; for, in A.
C. Ewing's words, 'to say that ethical concepts properly thought
out can provide an argument for believing in God is not the same
thing as to say that a reference to God is already included in the
definition of all ethical terms'.[4] Hastings Rashdall made the same
point thus : —

'Undoubtedly we must assert what is called the "independence"
of the moral judgment. The judgment "to love is better than to
hate" has a meaning complete in itself, which contains no
reference whatever to any theological presupposition. It is a
judgment which is, and which can intelligibly be, made by people
of all religions or of none. But we may still raise the question
whether the validity of that judgment can be defended without
theological implications.'[5]

We shall be helped towards understanding the position that
Rashdall and Ewing hold if we bear in mind two truths that are
constantly relevant to theological discussions : the distinction
between the order of being and the order of knowing (the *ordo
essendi* and the *ordo cognoscendi*); and the 'relative independence'
or 'derived autonomy' of the created order.

The first of these distinctions is one that critics of natural
theology frequently forget. In the order of being the Creator takes
absolute precedence over every creature. He is the fount of all
reality, the source from whom every aspect of finite being flows.
But in the order of knowing he does not come first. We are immediately aware of creatures and creaturely activities. It needs a
deliberate act of will to discern God in and beyond them as their
constant ground.

[4] *Prospect for Metaphysics* (London 1961, p. 46).
[5] *Philosophy and Religion* (London 1909, pp. 70-71). See also his *The
Theory of Good and Evil* (Vol. 2 Oxford 1907, pp. 206-13). Compare also
A. Macbeath's *Experiments in Living* (London 1952, p. 295).

Thus we are immediately aware of moral claims and values as facts existing 'in their own right'. They have their own distinctive meaning and validity. It needs additional perception to see in them the imprints of the God from whom they are derived. The task of the philosopher is to prompt this perception by pointing to those aspects of morality that demand a religious explanation. His aim is to show that what is first in the order of knowing is second in the order of being.

There is, as Ewing observes, a parallel to this procedure in the argument from design. The behaviour of organisms appears at first to be self-explanatory. When the biologist gives further 'explanations' he does so in terms of finite causes. But the theologian points to aspects of organic activity that demand the postulation of a divine Intelligence as their Final Cause. We are not aware of God when we contemplate the course of nature. If we were we should not need any argument to indicate his existence. At the same time certain aspects of the cosmic process (the co-operation of separate elements for the achievement of a single end, the pre-adaptation of material factors to mental life, the emergence of mind itself) point to God as the Prime Mover and Final Cause in the order of existence.

An understanding of the principle enunciated by Rashdall and Ewing is further facilitated by a consideration of what I have called the 'relative independence' or 'derived autonomy' of the created order. The paradox in these phrases is inevitable. It belongs to the very idea of creation. God, in making the world, gave it its own structure and laws. While being its ever-present first cause he chooses to govern it through secondary causes. Therefore while the world depends wholly on him for its existence it also enjoys a relative independence in so far as its modes of operation can be partially understood without any reference to him.

We are used to applying this distinction within the domain of the natural sciences. But it is no less applicable to the moral realm. Morality is autonomous in so far as we can recognize the meaning and validity of the right and the good without recourse to the idea of God; but the autonomy is derived in so far as moral claims and values cannot be explained until they are seen in the light of their divine origin. Alternatively, morality possesses a relative independence. Its distinctive nature and detailed contents can be known independently of religious faith;

but they cannot be metaphysically justified unless they are derived from the character and will of God.

Some Christian thinkers hold that the moral sense is itself an awareness of God. Thus John Baillie maintained that atheists who acknowledge the existence of unconditional obligation possess 'unconscious faith'; they confess God 'in the bottom of their hearts' though they deny him with 'the top of their minds'.[6] Similarly Maritain asserts that 'the good pagan' is a 'pseudo-atheist' who unconsciously 'knows' without 'recognizing' God.[7] According to this view every moral person is 'really' a believer even when he finds the idea of divine existence intellectually unacceptable.

No one who has had the privilege of friendship with a morally sensitive agnostic can fail to find this view attractive. It is especially telling in the case of those who once believed, then lost their faith, but still retain Christian sentiments. Yet the view is exposed to two grave objections.

Firstly, Baillie contradicts himself. He stated earlier that 'we cannot know anything without at the same time at least thinking we know something about it, because in the very moment that we are confronted with any reality, so becoming acquainted with it, our minds start to frame certain propositions concerning it'.[8] This seems to me to be true, and as true in religion as in any other sphere; but it is incompatible with the view that atheists know God when they reject all propositions concerning him.

Secondly, the view fails to observe the distinction between the *ordo essendi* and the *ordo cognoscendi*. God, we have seen, comes first in the order of being, but second in the order of knowing. To say that he is the origin of moral concepts is not to say that he is known as such. Conversely, to say that atheists do not know him is not to say that they lack all contact with him; for he is nearer to all creatures than they are to themselves, and he is especially near to those who obey his law.[9]

[6] *The Sense of the Presence of God* (Oxford 1962, pp. 79-87).

[7] *Approaches to God* (London 1955, p. 84).

[8] Op. cit. p. 16.

[9] Consequently I do not for a moment wish to deny the truth so splendidly expressed by St Augustine and Pascal that God is constantly seeking men through his prevenient, active, presence in the soul. But I do not see how they can *know* him until they have found him. Baillie gives

4. The moral argument must do justice to both the 'right' and the 'good'. These two concepts are distinct. They represent two different attitudes to the moral life. The first attitude is derived from Israel and is typified by the Mosaic law. The second is derived from Greece and is typified by Aristotle's *Nicomachean Ethics*. Both have penetrated the ethical thought of Western Christendom.

Much was written by British philosophers between the wars on the ways in which rightness and goodness are related. I cannot enter into this discussion which has been well summarized in a book by J. H. Muirhead.[10] I can only express my opinion that the discussion has shown the impossibility of reducing 'right' to 'good' or 'good' to 'right' within a purely moral setting. Both terms are needed for different purposes; but each, in the last resort, needs the other. Consequently the theist must weigh each separately when he is considering the moral evidence for religion.

At the same time I believe that theism can unify these concepts in a wholly new way. I have already claimed that 'God' acts as an explanatory word; but it also unifies what it explains. I hope to show later, in discussing the views of W. G. Maclagan, that unless we adopt the theistic postulate the unification of the right and the good is impossible.

5. The theistic inference must lead to a moral—not to a supra-moral or, even less, sub-moral—God. Unless God possesses supreme moral worth he cannot be the foundation of morality.

Because the members of the Homeric pantheon shared human frailties they could not inspire moral vision. Doubtless they possessed some claim to divinity, even by Christian standards, in so far as they were 'immortal'. Doubtless, too, for this reason they were capable of eliciting an admiration that is akin to awe. Yet their conduct fell below even average human standards. Therefore when Greek philosophers came to justify moral principles they did so on purely human grounds.

This picture admittedly requires modification. In the first place

his case away in his *Our Knowledge of God* (Oxford 1939, p. 64). There he supports his view by quoting the words of Jacob in Genesis 28. 16-17: 'Surely the Lord is in this place, and I knew it not; this is none other but the house of God, and this is the gate of heaven'. Yet the whole point of these verses is that while God was present Jacob did *not* know him.

[10] *Rule and End in Ethics* (Oxford 1932).

even the gods, however capricious they might be, were bound by a moral order represented by such concepts as *Dike, Nemesis,* and *Moira.* Furthermore many of them (especially Zeus) were gradually moralized by poets and philosophers.[11] But on both these points we see morality acting as an independent force that purifies religion; and it was only after such purification had taken place that morality could receive a theistic sanction.

It would be equally invalid to draw an inference to the a-moral, or supra-moral, God of some monistic systems. Ethics cannot be derived from an Absolute in which the differences between good and evil disappear. Whether such an undifferentiated ground of cosmic unity can properly be called God or become the object of true worship is highly doubtful. It is at any rate certain that he (or it) cannot satisfy the moral consciousness which rests on the conviction that good and evil cannot be resolved in any kind of higher synthesis.

God, then, must be wholly good. He must perfectly exemplify all the qualities which we know to be binding on us in our human life. Otherwise he cannot be the source of moral obligation.

The God of the Bible satisfies this requirement. From the first he is a moral being who makes moral demands on his worshippers. When he revealed himself to Moses he also gave the law by which his people were to live. The very word for 'law' in Hebrew (*torah*) has inescapably theistic implications. It is the 'teaching' or 'instruction' given by God to Israel. But the law is not merely the enactment of God's will; it is also the reflection of his nature. Hence its culminating formula is: 'You shall be holy, for I am holy.' The 'end' of 'the good life' (to use Greek terms) is to imitate divine perfection.[12]

[11] Christopher Dawson sees this as an instance of a fundamental principle. 'Behind the anthropomorphic divinities and the visible powers of nature there was the abstract conception of cosmic order or divine law —such as *Rita* in India, *Asha* in Persia, the Greek *Dike* and *Moira* and the Chinese *Tao*—out of which the gods emerged by mythology and ritual and into which they were re-absorbed by philosophy and theology' (*Religion and Culture,* London 1949, p. 146).

[12] T. W. Manson summed up the essence of Hebrew ethics thus. 'The last ground of moral obligation is the command of God; and the supreme ideal is the imitation of a God who is at once king and father, who exhibits in the field of nature and history, and above all in his dealings with Israel, the qualities of holiness and righteousness, mercy and faithfulness, love and covenant-loyalty, which are to be the pattern for the

It would, of course, be false to say that the Jews achieved a full and consistent apprehension of God's perfection. Sometimes they understood his holiness (his *mysterium tremendum et fascinans*) in non-moral terms, even after Isaiah's insistence that his holiness is neither more nor less than righteousness in its highest mode. Sometimes too they interpreted God's moral attitudes anthropomorphically, especially when they endowed him with their own vindictiveness. In ethical, as in other, ways God's revelation under the old covenant was not pure and complete; it was limited by the capacities of its recipients; and these limitations were not removed until God gave us a direct image of himself by assuming our nature in Jesus Christ.

In the light of Christ we see that God is self-existent goodness. His essence and existence are identical. At first sight these abstract assertions may seem to be far removed from the personal images of the Bible. In fact they are metaphysical axioms on which the Biblical union of faith and ethics rests. A simple exposition of their moral relevance may be given thus.

When we look at the goodness of finite persons we see that it constitutes their essential form (that which, in both a deontological and a teleological sense, they 'ought' to be). Yet their goodness is distinct from their existence in two ways. Firstly, they might never have existed. We can imagine a person who has every virtue so that his essence is complete; but he lacks real existence. In the finite order 'to be good' does not entail 'to be'. Secondly, no human person can say that his existence corresponds completely to his essence. We are all 'on the way' to goodness. Sins still have to be conquered, temptations set aside, and new heights of virtue scaled.

By contrast God's essence and existence are identical. It is untrue to say that his goodness might not have existed; for he exists necessarily. Equally it is untrue to say that his existence falls short of goodness; for his goodness is perfect and unchanging. We are not to think of his goodness as in any way distinct from the act whereby he is; for this act is the eternal actualization of a goodness that is underived and infinite. Therefore his secondary and particular acts of will in relation to his creatures are inevitably good.

behaviour of his subjects and children' (*Ethics and the Gospel*, London 1960, p. 18).

39

Admittedly Christian moralists have sometimes obscured, if not denied, these basic truths. They have divorced God's essence from his existence and, correlatively, his nature from his will. They have then appealed to his will as something which merits our obedience apart from its congruence with our moral insight. On this view an action is right simply and solely because God commands it.[13]

The view is a clear instance of the naturalistic fallacy. It is an attempt to derive moral notions from a non-moral premiss; for the premiss is non-moral although it is theistic. A divine will that is not morally interpreted is logically on a par with any other non-moral premiss (such as pleasure) from which duty is derived.

It is doubtful whether there has ever been a completely consistent 'theological naturalist'. At some point everyone judges the will of God in the light of independently known moral principles. Thus it would be hard to find a Christian who was prepared to assert that it is right to exterminate one's enemies solely because this is sometimes commanded by God in the Old Testament. If it should be said that our change of outlook is due to the fact that we have a higher revelation of God in Christ it must be replied that we judge this revelation to be higher because it appeals to our highest moral sensibilities.

Since God is goodness the person who seeks to do God's will can never ask 'why *ought* I to be good?' The question is nonsensical. Goodness is self-justifying. So also is the obligation to pursue it. The only difference between the theist and the atheist on this score is that while the atheist is content with a *human* ideal of goodness the theist affirms that such an ideal is inadequate unless it is understood as a created likeness of the uncreated goodness which is God.

Yet there remain the religious sanctions that Christians have attached to duty—the hope of heaven and the fear of hell. I shall return to this question in chapter five. Here it is enough to contrast extrinsic and intrinsic sanctions.

A sanction is extrinsic when it differs in kind from the action that it follows. Prizes and punishments are (as a rule) in this category. The book which the schoolboy gets for his excellence

---

[13] Thus Paley defined 'right' as 'consistency with the will of God'. Paley's naturalism and Whately's objections to it are summarized by A. N. Prior (*Logic and the Basis of Ethics*, Oxford 1949, pp. 100-02).

in physics is not homogeneous with his work in the class-room or laboratory. The prison-sentence which the embezzler receives is not homogeneous with his crime. The same sentence under the same conditions could be served by other men for very different crimes.

A sanction is intrinsic when it embodies the consequences of an act in terms that are homogeneous with the act itself. Thus the schoolboy could be told that the 'true' or 'lasting' prize for his industry is the knowledge he has gained. Similarly the embezzler could be told that his greatest penalty is his sense of shame. In recognizing intrinsic sanctions to be morally higher than extrinsic ones we follow Plato who in his *Republic* described the external rewards of virtue only after he had shown that justice intrinsically benefits the soul.

It is obvious that the only sanctions permitted even to religion are those which are intrinsic to morality. They must affirm the consequences of good and evil in terms that are congruous with ethical autonomy.[14] The language of rewards and penalties is no more than a metaphorical means of stating that in a world directed by a just and loving God virtue is as bound to result in happiness as vice in misery. The happiness is that which attends devotion to good 'for its own sake'; the misery is that which attends deliberate acts of wickedness. 'Heaven' is a life spent endlessly with the Goodness which is God; 'hell' is exclusion from the good for ever. And just as no one can attain to heavenly bliss unless he has learned to love goodness in itself, so no one can avoid the pains of hell unless he has learned to hate evil in itself.

The moralist is equally obliged to reject extrinsically conceived religious sanctions when they are put forward as a ground for ensuring the welfare of society. The mere suggestion that Christianity is to be advocated because it restrains people from socially undesirable behaviour undermines the integrity of both morality and religion. The only valid reason for believing in God is that the belief is seen to be true; and the only valid reason for doing or not doing X is that X is seen to be good or evil, right or wrong. Preachers and politicians who appeal to Christian faith

---

[14] For an uncompromising condemnation of religious rewards which are extrinsic to morality see K. E. Kirk's *The Threshold of Ethics* (London 1952, pp. 21-26).

as the only 'support' for 'declining moral standards' would do well to reflect that the maxim *expedit esse deos* was coined by a pagan cynic.

I shall summarize this section by considering two statements that Christian writers sometimes make. The first is that 'morality cannot be objective unless it has a religious ground'. The second is that 'morality depends on religion'.

1. I have maintained that goodness and rightness are self-evidently objective. We can perceive their normative character and their embodiment in human wills without religious faith. Indeed faith presupposes this perception. Unless our moral ideas are capable of being objective in the second and third senses that I gave we could not have any grounds for believing that they are also objective ontologically; for we could never know that our moral descriptions of ultimate reality are correct.

Naturally our belief in moral norms receives a new, and metaphysically final, confirmation if we believe that they are grounded in a God who created and directs the world. This confirmation will be especially compelling if we believe that Christ is God incarnate; for we shall then see in a human life the immediate stamp of divine perfection. I shall develop this truth—for I believe it to be the ultimate truth for ethics—in my closing chapter.

My sole contention now is a negative one. Moral norms do not *qua* norms entail divine existence. It is conceivable that if God did not exist they would have the universality they now possess. All we need assume is a common human nature and the fact of obligation. We can maintain (as I shall do) that in being obligatory norms require the theistic postulate; but we cannot argue (so far as I can see) that their universal character requires it.

2. I have, I hope, made clear the sense in which I consider morality to be dependent on religion. There is no necessity for dependence within the *ordo cognoscendi*; for the atheist can grasp the meaning and objectivity of moral terms. It is invalid to maintain cognitive dependence by resorting to the contradictory idea of 'unconscious faith'.

Yet, it may be said, surely the *believer* derives *some* moral judgments from theological premisses. Thus a pacifist could affirm that because God is love and has commanded us to love our enemies it must be wrong to oppose them with armed force. But the premiss of this affirmation presupposes that the speaker knows what is meant by 'love', and the conclusion presupposes that he know (or thinks he knows) the bearing of love on international relationships.

However, in the *ordo essendi* the moral life (together with created life in all its other forms) depends on God. In the succeeding chapters I shall give reasons for affirming this dependence; but I trust that nothing I shall say will violate the principle of ethical autonomy within the *ordo cognoscendi*.

If, then, these principles are observed what kind of validity can the moral argument possess? One thing must be said at once. *All* the so-called 'proofs' are bound to fail if they are taken as step-by-step demonstrations. It is impossible to construct a formal syllogism in which the mind moves with deductive certainty from non-theistic premisses to divine existence.

If the proofs are to have any cogency they must rest on a frank recognition of three facts.

1. The initial concept of God in Christian theism is derived from Biblical revelation. Thus Aquinas defined God in terms of Exodus 3. 14 where Yahweh is described as 'He Who Is (*Qui Est*).' Aquinas took this translation of the divine name to mean that God is the self-existent, infinite, Creator. His starting-point was given by faith. Philosophical, no less than dogmatic, theology is the activity of *fides quaerens intellectum*.

2. Since the Christian idea of God is based on revelation and since his existence cannot be formally deduced, we must understand the proofs in an *in*formal way. This, to adopt the word chosen by E. L. Mascall,[15] is the way of 'contuition'. Every proof invites us to 'contuit' God and the world—to view them together so that we shall see God as Creator of the world and the world as dependent on God. Every proof seeks to explicate the 'cosmological idea' that even the simplest mind can grasp prephilosophically.

3. In treating any element in the natural evidence for theism it is therefore necessary to maintain a balance between two truths.

(a) The evidence genuinely points to God. It is a sign, or indication, of him. The theist claims that finite experience in all

---

[15] *Words and Images* (London 1957, pp. 84-7).

its modes cannot be ultimately explained unless God is posited as its source. The idea of God is therefore rational, and the arguments used to establish his existence are rational, in the ratiocinative sense of reason that is signified by the scholastic *ratio*. Discursive thought—'thinking about', 'offering explanations', 'giving reasons for', 'solving problems'—has an essential part to play.

(b) At the same time discursive reason (*ratio*) cannot itself compel assent to the truth of the theistic postulate. There is always a 'gap' which it cannot cross between any ground for faith and faith itself. When due allowance has been made for exaggeration existentialists are right in calling the act of faith a 'leap' and in contrasting the objective deficiency of the evidence with the certitude of the believer. When *ratio* has done its work as thoroughly as it can it must leave the final apprehension to *intellectus*—to the mind's capacity for intuiting God in (or contuiting him with) his effects.

4. This final intuition cannot occur unless there is at least some degree of spiritual experience. Even the cosmological proof (which may seem to be the most abstract of the proofs) presupposes wonder and humility. The religious sense (if only in a confused and nascent form) is even more obviously required by the moral proof. This point was strongly stated by A. E. Taylor thus:—

'The witness of conscience to the active reality of the living God is the evidence of *fact*. It converts belief in God from a mere "theistic hypothesis" into the faith which is the *evidence* of things not seen. But the force of this evidence will naturally be under-estimated by the thoughtless and the self-satisfied; one may doubt whether it is ever disclosed in its full strength to any man who has never from the bottom of his heart uttered the cry, "God be merciful to me a sinner".'[16]

This, then, is the framework in which I wish to place the moral argument. This argument (like every other) is persuasive, not demonstrative. But I realize even so that theism may appear to be untenable for the following reason.

Christian theism affirms that God is incomprehensible. We can

[16] *Does God Exist?* (London 1947, pp. 120-1).

never know him (in this life) as he is. We can know him only by analogy with created being. It is always true for all of us that 'now we see in a mirror dimly, but then face to face'. How then can God be said to 'explain' anything at all? How can he be brought within the scope of rational theology? While a full answer to these questions would require a separate study in religious language I believe that we shall be helped greatly if we remember four principles.

(a) An *explicans* need not be clearer than the *explicandum*. Many scientific hypotheses are partial mysteries. Those used by depth-psychology furnish an example. The symptoms of the patient are observable; but in explaining them the analyst is obliged to postulate non-observable activities; and since the latter are unconscious they can be described only by analogy with the activities of the conscious mind.

(b) The obscurity which surrounds moral concepts and demands a theistic explanation differs in kind from the obscurity which we find in God. The first obscurity is a 'puzzle' to which we feel there ought to be an 'answer'. The second obscurity brings the sense of awe, not puzzlement—the awe produced by the sheer fact of self-existent Being.

(c) The absolute mystery of God is not, even from the standpoint of philosophy, a defect (something which we should *like* to make absolutely plain). On the contrary it is the condition of his capacity to act as a final *explicans*. He cannot be the cause of finite phenomena unless he himself is uncaused (that is, unless his essence is identical with his existence in an incomprehensible way).

(d) Perhaps the completeness of our ignorance concerning God 'in himself' will remain an obstacle to belief even if the preceding principles are endorsed. But no one can expect to be convinced of God's reality without a *personal* response. Everyone must feel the theistic postulate as something that his own moral life requires. Otherwise it is impossible to apprehend God with 'real assent'. Moreover this feeling (as the quotation from A. E. Taylor showed) is unlikely to occur without a religious sense of need.

One thing, at any rate, seems to me to be completely clear on purely rational grounds. *If* God exists it is only the Christian idea of him that can satisfy both religion and morality. If God is to satisfy the moral consciousness he must be good; for a supra-moral Power could not justify an objective difference between good and evil, right and wrong. Also, from the religious standpoint, God must be personal; for the idea of an impersonal God would not add anything to the idea of an impersonal 'moral order'.

Furthermore, God must be *absolutely* good. Since moral claims are unconditional they show that if God is their source his goodness is unconditioned or infinite; for we could not give our unreserved allegiance to a being whose goodness suffered from our finite limitations. It is not enough for him to be good in this or that respect, or to this or that degree. He must be the sum of all perfections.

Now if God is infinite in goodness he must be infinite in existence. An existentially finite God would still exhibit goodness in a finite form; he would still be aware of participating in a goodness with which he was not identical, even though he embodied it spontaneously and to a supreme degree; and so, being conditioned in his actualization of the good, he could not promulgate it *in his own name* as an unconditional command.

What does it mean to say that God is infinitely existent? It means, quite simply, that he is free from the limitations that affect our own existence. Among these limitations particularity and change are those that struck Plato most forcibly. But through and beyond these two there is the fact of sheer contingency. There is no reason in ourselves why we should exist. Our essence is under the constant threat of non-existence. Since we exist we shall (perhaps) be good (though only partly good and only good in this way or that); but if we did not exist there would be no substance in which our goodness could inhere. The only unconditioned essence would be one that exists necessarily. God's goodness therefore must be self-existent if it is to possess the unconditioned character that it must have if it is to be the personal source of unconditional claims.

Yet not even a God who was self-existent Goodness could morally demand our complete obedience unless he was also our Creator. His goodness would be unconditioned; but he would not have the right to issue unconditional commands. He would have this right only if we owed our existence to his creative act. Unless he made us in our entirety he could not demand the total surrender of our lives that the moral law requires.[17]

I fully realize that the proof of God's self-existence and creative power can be more directly established through the cosmological argument.[18] But I believe that all the theistic arguments ultimately indicate these truths. Once the human mind embarks on theistic speculation it cannot find rest in any lesser goal. In my fourth chapter I shall suggest that when morality is placed on a cosmic setting it converges on other arguments and joins with them in pointing to the same uncreated, eternal, wholly good Reality.

At the same time I believe that the moral argument has four distinctive merits.

Firstly, its data are of immediate concern to everyone. We are all familiar, to some extent and at some level, with the problems posed by good and evil, right and wrong. I do not mean that the data adduced by the other proofs necessarily seem irrelevant. But their relevance is not so immediately apparent, partly because their terms are more abstract, and partly because they presuppose a contemplative attitude to nature that is hard to acquire in our technologically conditioned age.

Secondly, if morality is objective in the senses I have given it introduces us immediately to an intelligible world beyond the world of space and time. We need not subscribe to Kant's separation of noumena from phenomena to see that while man is (on his material side) a part of nature his conscience belongs to a realm that both transcends nature and, in a measure, governs it. Religion clarifies and deepens the spiritual environment to which morality by nature testifies.

Thirdly, for this reason the moral sense is nearer than any other to the 'sense of the divine'. In distinguishing between these two senses I have said that it is necessary for the first to be completed in the second. Sooner or later we must become aware of God's reality through a distinctively religious sense of need. I hope to show how this need is implied by the obedience due to moral claims.

[17] Of course if we already believe that God's existence is infinite it follows by a logical necessity that he is also the Creator; for he could not be conditioned by anything that pre-exists him; but I am here concerned with the possibility of establishing his creativity on *moral* grounds.
[18] For a learned and persuasive formulation of this argument see E. L. Mascall's *He Who Is* (London 1943).

The last and strongest reason for pursuing the moral argument as far as it will take us is that it was through the law (*torah*) that God revealed himself to Israel. If, therefore, we are to 'philosophize in faith' we shall look to the moral life as cogent evidence for God. Just as it was through Moses and the prophets that God disclosed the secret of his being to the people of his covenant so it is, as by a reflected light, that he discloses himself to all men through the law that he has written on their hearts.

In the three following chapters I shall examine the theistic implications of morality under the concepts of Duty, Goodness, and Beatitude. In the last chapter I shall try to show how these created signs of God are fulfilled in Christian revelation.

Chapter 3

DUTY

At the end of chapter one I maintained that moral claims constitute an independent order of reality. I shall now suggest five reasons for inferring God as their source or ground.

1. Claims, I submit, are not self-explanatory. Their mode of existence is highly puzzling and obscure. We feel their 'pressure'; we are aware of being 'constrained' by them; but on the purely moral plane we are unable to give any further account of their existence. They just 'are'—enigmatic entities in an uncharted sphere. Their enigma consists in the fact that, taken in themselves, they are *impersonal*.

In order to perceive this ontological incongruity it is enough to consider ordinary language. The words 'obligation', 'duty', 'claim' always imply a *personal* constraint whenever they refer to an object within the finite world. We say that we are 'under an obligation' to our friend, but not to our computer.[1] Similarly we define justice as 'giving every man his due'; but we should consider it nonsensical to replace 'every man' by 'every*thing*'. The personal overtones of 'claim' are no less obvious. As W. D. Ross has put it, ' "claim" seems inevitably to suggest two persons, one of whom might make a claim on the other'.[2]

A personal reference is especially clear in 'law' when this is taken to signify 'command'.[3] It is impossible to think of a com-

---

[1] The fact that we doubt whether we have duties towards animals (even though we deplore cruelty towards them) is due to their ambiguous status. They are not (as Descartes thought) complex machines; but also they are not persons.
[2] *The Right and the Good* (Oxford 1946, p. 20).
[3] For the argument from the moral law to a divine Lawgiver see especially Clement Webb (*Divine Personality and Human Life*, London 1920, pp. 113-44). Webb acknowledges his debt to Martineau.

mand without also thinking of a commander.The analogy with positive law makes this plain. Of any such law it can be asked: 'what is its source and authority?' While the source may lie in a remote and unrecorded past, the present authority must be a person or group of persons who act as its interpreters—the Sovereign, Parliament, the judiciary.

A clear choice faces us. Either we take moral claims to be self-explanatory modes of *impersonal* existence or we explain them in terms of a personal God. The first of these alternatives cannot be disproved. The idea that claims can exist without any personal ground is not, perhaps, a logical contradiction; for even if in our experience of finite things and persons claims are always personal we cannot demonstrate that they must be personal *per se*. But we can say that if the transcendent and visible orders of morality are not continuous at this vital point—if the *modus essendi* of claims in themselves is totally different from their *modus essendi* when empirically embodied—the moral life is unintelligible.

If moral claims are left in this unintelligible state it is hard for a reflective person to continue believing in them; for belief is always insecure until it is rooted in understanding. *Credo ut intelligam.* Consequently Illtyd Trethowan has said: 'moral obligation, as I see it, is so far from being self-explanatory that if it were not made intelligible by being found in a metaphysical —and in fact a theistic-context, I should be greatly tempted to hand it over to the anthropologists and the psychologists'.[4]

The truth in Trethowan's statement is that while naturalistic explanations of the moral law fail to account for its authority they at least do justice to its *personal* character. The dictates of society cannot explain the absoluteness of the categorical imperative; but in so far as they are personal they have a superficial credibility. On the other hand bare belief in an impersonal order of claims, while it is compatible with their absolute authority, does not provide the personal basis which their imperatival quality requires.[5]

I shall now deal with three objections to my argument.

4 *The Basis of Belief* (London 1960, p. 117).
5 For a brief, but forceful, statement of the view that the categorical imperative must be a *personal* constraint see A. R. Vidler's *Christian Belief* (London 1950, pp. 20-21). Compare also G. F. Wood's *Theological Explanation* (London 1958, pp. 190-92).

(a) It has been said that those who argue from the moral law to a divine Lawgiver assume too readily that language mirrors facts. It is invalid to say 'because Western languages take the subject-predicate form the world must consist in substances and their attributes'. It is no more valid to say 'because law suggests a lawgiver, a divine lawgiver must exist'.

The example is misleading. The move from subject-predicate to substance-attribute is one from language to reality; but the move from human claimants to a divine Claimant occurs within reality itself. Certainly the belief in a divine lawgiver involves an analogical use of moral terms; but this use is governed by a desire to unify the facts to which these terms refer. The argument is that since within the human realm claims imply a claimant and laws a lawgiver the same implications must be posited within the supra-human order if we are to make morality consistent.

(b) A second objection is that belief in a divine lawgiver is merely the projection of an authoritarian 'father-image'. The Christian illicitly transfers authority from an earthly to a heavenly father when he posits God as the source of the moral law. Once he sees the transference for what it is a sign of emotional immaturity—he will be able to discard it and give his ethics a purely humanistic foundation.

A full answer would require a critique of the whole Freudian attitude towards religion. Here I shall simply observe that the objection is a gross *petitio principii*. If it is logically possible that the authority ascribed to God is solely a 'projection' it is no less logically possible that the authority of human fathers is derived from that of the divine Father 'from whom every family in heaven and on earth is named'.[6]

(c) It could be objected that the personal source of positive laws does not itself make them valid. Even a technically legitimate ruler forfeits his right to obedience if his mandates do not correspond to moral norms. So John Laird, in rejecting Clement Webb's argument for a divine Lawgiver, wrote: 'it is not apparent that the *rightness* or *equity* of any juridical law is just what the sovereign commands, and so that if there were no commander there could be no such thing as justice or equity'.[7]

[6] Eph. 3. 15.
[7] *Mind and Deity* (London 1941, p. 231).

Laird's criticism can be briefly answered. Of course the commands of human rulers may be morally invalid because they may be wicked or foolish men. But God's commands are always right and true because he himself *is* perfect righteousness and truth. Laird assumes (as so many critics of ethical theism do) that every theologian is a victim of the naturalistic fallacy.

Yet I must clarify (even at the cost of repetition) what I mean by saying that personal theism 'explains' the ontological objectivity of moral claims. There can be no hope of making the ground of duty 'plain' in a form that would imply an intuition of God's essence. The most the theist can maintain is that the idea of a divine Lawgiver elucidates the *modus essendi* of claims according to the limits of analogical predication.

The agnostic, of course, may find the very idea of analogy unacceptable. If we cannot know God 'in himself' how can we invoke him as an *explicans*? I have already anticipated this objection by suggesting firstly that an *explicans* need not be clearer than the *explicandum*, and secondly that the obscurity (when understood as the 'mystery') of God is the condition of his capacity to act as a final *explicans*. Two further considerations must be stressed.

Firstly, the main task of metaphysics is to offer ultimate explanations of facts which are not self-explanatory either when taken in themselves or even when related to each other. If someone does not desire this type of explanation he cannot be compelled to seek it. To some people 'ultimate explanations' will always seem gratuitous. The theist has no magic formula for dealing with an anti-metaphysical attitude. His only hope of dispelling it is to show the contradictions it involves. If the atheist is content to acquiesce in these the argument is at an end.

Secondly, since theism is a secondary pursuit it is likely to seem chimerical if it is severed from its experiential roots. When we look at claims theoretically we may not perhaps be over-worried by the problem of their status; but the problem cannot be so easily evaded when we recollect their practical significance. *Theoria* without *praxis* is empty, and *praxis* without *theoria* is blind.

2. The contradiction I have pointed out becomes especially apparent (and distressing) when we consider the *obedience* that the categorical imperative requires. Here we have an additional

paradox. On the one hand claims transcend every human person and every personal embodiment. On the other hand we value the personal more highly than the impersonal; so that it is contradictory to assert that impersonal claims are entitled to the allegiance of our wills. The only solution of the paradox is to suppose that the order of claims, while it appears as impersonal from a purely moral point of view, is in fact rooted in the personality of God.

This demand for personality in the object of obedience is confirmed by the manner in which abstract claims are conditioned in their modes of operation by a personal setting. Two modes of conditioning are plain.

In the first place claims are apt to be most stringent when they are personally mediated. Thus for many readers the claims of loyalty in general and promise-keeping in particular are exemplified supremely in their marriage-vows. Conversely the violation of another person's trust incurs universal condemnation. Certainly it is always wrong to break one's word, or even to intend to do so, except in order to observe some other claim. Yet we feel especial guilt when our wrong-doing betrays another person's confidence. From the Christian standpoint all wrongdoing takes this form; for it is, directly or indirectly, a betrayal of God's love.[8]

Secondly, in cases of conflict between claims most of us, I believe, would give preference to the claim which possessed the greater *personal* stringency. At least we should tend to do so. The most quoted instance is the dilemma created by a conflict between the demands of truth-telling and compassion. Many of those who have a high regard for truth would be prepared to tell a lie in order to save a sick friend from harmful, or even unnecessary, distress. Adherence to abstract principles at *any* cost merits the reproach of hardness if not also inhumanity.

3. I have been speaking of the especial weight that we attach to claims when they occur within personal relationships. Yet persons do not merely exemplify abstract claims. They exert claims in their own right because they are persons and not things. Even the atheist admits this truth when he agrees with Kant that

---

[8] Hence the words in the greatest of the penitential Psalms (51. 4): 'against thee, thee only, have I sinned, and done this evil in thy sight'.

each person must be treated as an end and never simply as a means.

It is on this ground that we condemn the subordination of the individual to the State. For certain purposes a person can be viewed in terms of his official role or social class. Yet he also has *intrinsic* worth. He deserves unlimited respect solely because he is a human being. This respect can be neither increased nor diminished by his role or status in society.

An admirable statement of this moral truth from agnostic premisses has been given by J. P. Corbett.

'I have come to realize clearly, lately at least, that life is intolerable unless you recognize your neighbour as a person who has absolute claims upon you, unless you go about in the world meeting people and seeing in those people something which demands your utmost attention and all the service you can give them. This does not mean that you have to think in terms of any philosophical or religious system so far as I can see. It is just that it is only in unconditional service to the next man, whoever he may be, and under no matter what circumstances you meet him, that you escape from the sense of frustration and incompleteness and doubt which otherwise dogs one's steps.'[9]

It is instructive to compare and contrast this passage with another taken from Basil Willey's *Christianity Past and Present*.[10]

'Christianity teaches that humanity inevitably becomes subhuman when cut off from the superhuman; that, as Chesterton expressed it, nature becomes unnatural unless redeemed by the supernatural. It is indeed possible for an atheist to be noble, selfless, devoted to his fellows, and willing to lay down his life for them; we see examples of this around us constantly. But such nobility commonly has unconfessed religious springs, deep and hidden in the man's own heart or in his family history. It is theoretically indefensible except on religious presuppositions.'

I am here concerned solely to maintain that the belief in

[9] Taken from *The Listener* (January 21st, 1960). I am indebted to Trethowan (*op. cit.* p. 137) for the reference.
[10] Cambridge 1952, pp. 80-81.

human dignity is 'theoretically indefensible' unless it is derived from theistic premises. Whether it is practically tenable for any length of time without these premises is another question. But one cannot fail to be impressed by the fact (which Willey stresses) that many of the great Victorian humanists (such as T. H. Huxley and Leslie Stephen) were brought up in Christian homes.

There are, I believe, two reasons why human persons cannot *in themselves* exert the absolute claim of which Corbett speaks.

Firstly, each human person is a finite being and so exhibits goodness in a finite form. Most of us have some good qualities to some degree; but they are only partial embodiments of 'the good life'. One man excels in patience, another in courage, another in magnanimity; but none of us excels in all the virtues. Furthermore even if someone did possess all the virtues equally he would still not possess them to an infinite degree. The limitations of finite being would remain. Thus even Socrates exemplified the moral life in a typically Hellenic form. He himself would have said that nothing less than absolute goodness—the Idea of the Good that transcends all finite instances—can possess unconditioned worth.

Secondly, in fact (to anticipate the next stage of my argument) no one ever does exemplify all the virtues even in a finite mode. We are all sinners. How then can we merit reverence? Yet humanitarian sentiment compels the agnostic to treat all men as ends irrespective of their moral state. Hence, for example, he is shocked if the police maltreat a criminal in order to secure a conviction. One cannot evade the dilemma by saying that we are reverencing the 'ideal' of humanity, not the man himself; for firstly (as I shall later show) it is meaningless to speak of reverencing an 'ideal' (considered as a notion in the mind), and secondly we distinguish sharply between the reverence which is due to persons because they are persons and the admiration which we feel for them because they are good.

We are therefore driven to suppose that human persons exert their distinctive claim on account of their relation to a moral Absolute. Yet what can this relation be? There are three possibilities. Firstly we could say (with Hegel and Spinoza) that persons are 'modes' or 'expressions' of the Absolute; but a mode cannot possess the unconditioned nature of the Whole; and in any case the moral consciousness demands a God who transcends all finite selves. Secondly we may follow Kant in affirming that a person has dignity or worth in so far as he obeys (or is able to obey) the moral law. But (as I have already said) we revere persons even when they fail to obey the law and even if they are incapable of obedience.

We must therefore interpret the relation between human persons and the moral Absolute in terms of Christian theism. Their worth consists in the fact that they are created, loved, and destined for eternal life by God. The value we attach to them is the value bestowed on them by God; so that, in A. M. Farrer's words, 'what claims our regard is not simply our neighbour, but God in our neighbour and our neighbour in God'.[11] Human beings are 'sacred' because they are subject to the operations of God's holy will.

We see here another application of principles stated in the previous chapter. All creatures enjoy a 'relative independence' or 'derived autonomy'; but their ultimate significance lies in their relation to the Creator. In the order of knowing this relation is not immediately apparent; it must be grasped by faith. Yet whether it is grasped or not it persists as the ground of our moral attitudes and acts.

4. My fourth argument consists in the analysis of three moral terms: reverence, responsibility, and guilt.

(a) *Reverence.* Philosophers and theologians have often urged that our reverence for the moral law is an unacknowledged adoration of a holy law-giver. Thus Cook-Wilson affirmed that 'it is true that we speak of reverence for the moral law, but I believe no such feeling possible for a mere formula, and that, so far as it exists, it is only possible because we think of the moral law as a manifestation of the nature of the Eternal Spirit'.[12]

Although this argument impressed so acute a thinker as Cook-Wilson I find it, when taken alone, unconvincing. If 'reverence' means a 'sense of the sublime' it need not have a personal object in the moral, any more than in the natural, sphere. Equally if it means a 'sense of the numinous' it could still be compatible with a numinously toned apprehension of the moral law. Cook-

---

[11] *Faith and Logic* (London 1957, p. 26). The whole of Farrer's article is an important contribution to the moral argument.
[12] *Statement and Inference* Vol. 2. (Oxford 1926, p. 862).

Wilson's formulation of the argument appears to be convincing only because he has reduced the moral law to the status of a 'mere formula'.

However, if we take the moral law to mean an order of claims, and if we take reverence to include an attitude of devotion, the argument is a phenomenological form of the one I have already given. One cannot (morally) devote oneself to an object that is less than personal. The word 'reverence' would then describe the feeling-state that accompanies devotion and would not afford any independent evidence for theism.

(b) *Responsibility*. The concept of responsibility has clearer theistic implications. When we call someone 'irresponsible' we can often supply a reference to another human person. He is lacking in responsibility to (for example) his family or employers. To be responsible involves the idea of a person or persons to whom responsibility is due. Frequently 'being responsible' also conveys the sense of 'being answerable to'. Thus a minister of the Crown is answerable, or accountable, to Parliament for his decisions.

Yet we also speak of responsibility when no human persons are in view. Thus a person who wasted his talents could be called 'irresponsible'. Admittedly we may mean that he is irresponsible towards his wife who depends on his income or to his parents who are eager for his success. Yet even if he has no wife or parents, and even if he discharges the duties of his station to the satisfaction of society, we should still regard him as irresponsible if he squandered his gifts. To whom then is he responsible if not to God who bestows all gifts on trust?

The only other possibilities are that I am responsible either to myself or to an abstract order of claims. With regard to the first it seems to me plain that the idea of responsibility involves the idea of an 'other' to whom responsibility is due. Can then, this 'other' be a set of impersonal claims? Hardly. Each person must speak for himself. But I, for one, cannot make any sense of the view that such claims, however august and magisterial they may be, can be objects of responsibility. There is even a linguistic impropriety in saying that we are responsible to *it*.

(c) *Guilt*. The theistic implications of guilt were set forth by Newman with incomparable incisiveness as follows:—

'Inanimate things cannot stir our affections; these are correlative with persons. If, as is the case, we feel responsibility, are ashamed, are frightened, at transgressing the voice of conscience, this implies that there is One to whom we are responsible, before whom we are ashamed, whose claims upon us we fear. If, on doing wrong, we feel the same tearful, broken-hearted sorrow which overwhelms us on hurting a mother; if, on doing right, we enjoy the same sunny serenity of mind, the same soothing, satisfactory delight which follows on our receiving praise from a father, we certainly have within us the image of some person, to whom our love and veneration look, in whose smile we find our happiness, for whom we yearn, towards whom we direct our pleadings, in whose anger we are troubled and waste away. These feelings in us are such as require for their exciting cause an intelligent being : we are not affectionate towards a stone, nor do we feel shame before a horse or a dog; we have no remorse or compunction on breaking mere human law : yet, so it is, conscience excites all these painful emotions, confusion, foreboding, self-condemnation; and on the other hand it sheds upon us a deep peace, a sense of security, a resignation, and a hope, which there is no sensible, no earthly object to elicit. "The wicked flees, when no one pursueth"; then why does he flee? whence his terror? Who is it that he sees in solitude, in darkness, in the hidden chambers of his heart? If the cause of these emotions does not belong to this visible world, the Object to which his perception is directed must be Supernatural and Divine; and thus the phenomena of Conscience, as a dictate, avail to impress the imagination with the picture of a Supreme Governor, a Judge, holy, just, powerful, all-seeing, retributive, and is the creative principle of religion, as the Moral Sense is the principle of ethics.'[13]

Newman intended this to be a persuasive, not a demonstrative, argument. He simply points out that if in the finite and visible sphere our sense of guilt is proportionate to our betrayal of human persons, and if in this sphere we never find the same sense engendered by reflection on our treatment of mere 'things', we may reasonably conclude that our shame at having violated

---

[13] *A Grammar of Assent* (London 1901, pp. 109-10). This argument is developed (through an unusually profound analysis of moral guilt) by A. E. Taylor (*The Faith of a Moralist*, London 1930, Vol. 1, chap. 5).

the moral law is due to the fact that we are in the presence of a holy lawgiver.

5. My final argument is based on the fact of moral failure. Many of us find that we are unable to do what the law requires. We are faced with a distressing paradox. On the one hand 'I ought' theoretically implies 'I can'. On the other hand we often find that we can*not*. This inner conflict was described with classical simplicity by St Paul in Romans 7. 19: 'I do not do the good I want, but the evil I do not want is what I do.'

Certainly this conflict sometimes terminates in a moral victory. Thus I may be tempted to 'forget' a promise to attend a tedious meeting; but after a struggle I decide to go. Moreover it is undeniable that the highest acts of heroism can be performed from a sheer sense of duty in defiance of all selfish inclinations. It would be outrageous to set *a priori* limits to the moral possibilities of any particular person on any particular occasion.

Yet can anyone honestly say that he is able to perform the more exacting claims continually with the purity of motive that the moral law requires?[14] Or must we not admit that in our attempts to answer the absolute claim that our neighbour exerts on our regard we are constantly frustrated by a self-centredness that we are powerless to eradicate? If we admit this we posit a contradiction in the highest reaches of the moral life.

It is surely obvious that on the human plane the contradiction is insoluble. If our natures are defective how can they be healed except by aid which is strictly *super*natural? That such aid (or grace) is given through Christ is the gospel ('the good news') that the New Testament proclaims.

I shall not discuss this argument further for two reasons. Firstly, it is different in kind from my previous arguments which all consist in the theistic implications of the moral law *per se*; and it is on these implications that I wish to rest my case. Secondly, it could (I know) be said that we are obliged to perform only those actions (or cultivate only those attitudes) which lie within our power. We are not obliged to pursue perfection or even to aim at a standard which, though less than perfect, is

---

[14] Note how in Romans 7 St Paul illustrates his point by a commandment that involves an *interior* act—'Thou shalt not covet'. The essence of the moral life consists in the goodness of a *will* that is determined by (or is in accordance with) the moral law.

beyond our grasp. I shall comment on this view in chapter five. Meanwhile I merely wish to note that Jesus unquestionably required perfection, and that Christians regard the requirement as ethically self-evident; for Jesus came to fulfil, not to destroy, the *lex naturae*.

The argument to a divine Claimant and Lawgiver has recently been criticized in detail by W. G. Maclagan.[15] Since I shall be differing radically from him I wish to begin by expressing my admiration, not only for the skill with which he has presented his own case, but also for the clarity with which he has stated the fundamental questions that arise in any attempt to relate ethics to theology.

Maclagan objects to the argument on two grounds.

Firstly, the idea of a divine Lawgiver is meaningless. Maclagan starts with these alternatives. Either an action is right because God commands it or God commands it because it is right. The first alternative is morally, and the second theologically, disastrous; for according to the first an action becomes right or wrong by an arbitrary *fiat*, while according to the second, norms of rightness exist independently of God in whom they are supposed to have their ground. But there is a third possibility. 'God's action, it could be said, ceases to appear arbitrary without being conditioned by anything other than himself if moral distinctions are regarded neither as the product of his will nor as altogether independent of him, but as constitutive of his understanding, and as "having reality" only thus' (p. 70). Maclagan rejects this possibility for one reason only. 'What we know and our knowing it are from the human point of view never the same thing, and to claim knowledge that something is the case includes the affirmation that it is the case apart from our knowledge' (p. 70).

However, divine and human understanding are bound to differ at this point. To say that God knows what is absolutely right and good is to say, ultimately, that he knows himself; for he *is* goodness. Moral distinctions are constitutive of his understanding because moral values are constitutive of his being. Of course anyone can deny that essence and existence are identical in God; but the denial undermines Christian theism as a whole and not

[15] *The Theological Frontier of Ethics* (London, Allen & Unwin, 1961). In my discussion of Maclagan's views all my references are to this book.

simply the moral argument. I shall return to this point in the next chapter when discussing Maclagan's account of values. Meanwhile I shall concentrate on his second criticism.

In the second place he denies that there is any need to posit a divine Lawgiver. 'What we have to say is, rather, that the moral law is a law without a lawgiver; and to the objection that this is absurd the answer is that it is just a way of saying that to call it "law" at all is only inadequate metaphor for something that is *sui generis*' (p. 73).

To this I would make a three-fold reply.

(a) The metaphor of 'law' is an inevitable way of interpreting morality. Even as children we are aware of 'Thou shalt' (or, more often, 'Thou shalt not') as a mandate that is qualitatively distinct from both our parents' will and our own desires. At the rarefied level of philosophical speculation we have Kant's determinative example. When he came to describe moral 'autonomy'—that which differentiates moral activity from other activities and makes morality (as Maclagan puts it) *sui generis*—he did so through the concept of the 'categorical imperative'. Maclagan himself entitles the chapter from which I have quoted 'The Moral Demand'.

(b) Since the metaphor of law is inevitable is it not better to have it whole than maimed? Kant at any rate thought so when he affirmed that the goal of the practical reason is to see all duties as divine commands. So too Wordsworth called Duty 'the stern daughter of the voice of God'. Unless we posit God's existence the metaphor is defective at the core (not simply in some peripheral association).

(c) Maclagan anyhow misrepresents the theistic case by concentrating on the merely linguistic aspect of the inference to a divine Lawgiver. Even if (as I do not think possible) we discard the metaphor of 'law' we still have to explain the 'pressure' of moral claims. Maclagan does not offer any explanation. He simply leaves us with a mysterious 'demand'. This demand, he says, 'comes to us in the form of a duty—consciousness that imposes an absolute claim on our lives' (p. 53); it has unquestionable authoritativeness' (p. 55). These statements raise metaphysical questions which Maclagan does not even attempt to answer. On the contrary (as we shall see later) he confesses that the moral demand presupposes an 'order of values' concerning which nothing further can be said.

Since Maclagan wishes to reject a theistic inference from moral claims and to retain the possibility of belief in divine existence he is unable to give a satisfactory account of the relation between God and the moral law. Morality does not require a personal God. The moral consciousness can admit the idea of such a God only by equating him with the idea of an impersonal moral law. 'It is the moral experience that interprets to us (that is to say, that contributes to the interpretation of) the term "God", not the other way round' (p. 94). Yet Maclagan admits that religious experience requires a personal God. The only way out of this dilemma is to regard God as personal for some purposes and impersonal for others : —

'We must, then, somehow think of God as both personal and impersonal, and in one sense, it would seem, this presents no difficulty. Something very like it is achieved constantly, by all except the most simple-minded, in the very acknowledgement that personality as we know it does not adequately represent the divine nature. Yet when, in reflection, we endeavour to be more explicit, what results seems not to be integration so much as a sort of working conflation of the ideas of the personal and the impersonal, consisting in what remains the blank affirmation of their conjunction together with their use as *alternatives*, according as one or other seems more apt in a particular context. The concept of God (if it can be called a concept) then functions in much the same way as Eddington's notorious concept (if it can be called a concept) of "wavicle" in the theory of light. Now this procedure may be pragmatically justified; it may be indispensable for the 'practical purposes' of the religious life. Indeed it is, in a manner, preferable even as theory to any one-sided clarity. None the less it is manifestly unsatisfactory. Our working conflation rests on an inattention to the conflict of personal and impersonal conceptions rather than on a transcendence of it. What is needed is that we should, so to put it, replace a "bi-focal" vision of God by one that is "uni-focal".' (p. 179).

It seems to me that belief in God on these terms would be

metaphysically unjustified even if it is psychologically possible. Divine personality utterly transcends its created image. Yet to say that God is more that personal in the finite sense is one thing; but to say that he is impersonal is quite another. Furthermore (with reference to Eddington's 'wavicle') if there is one thing to be learned from empiricist critics of religion it is surely that theistic statements become untenable as soon as they are reduced to the pragmatic status of scientific postulates.

Maclagan treats the argument from claims to Claimant similarly. 'Claim', like 'law', is a metaphor that must not be pressed. But in speaking of claims he makes a statement I shall discuss because the misapprehensions it contains may be (at least partly) responsible for the precarious view he holds. 'I maintain,' he writes on p. 75, 'that there is no awareness of any such relationship [sc. between claims and God] inherent in the duty-consciousness itself, and I suggest that those who think there is do so precisely because they are not successfully abstracting from their independent theistic conviction. Their moral phenomenology has, so to put it, been vitiated by infection from beliefs at which they have arrived by a quite different route.'

Two observations must be made.

Firstly, Maclagan fails to observe the distinction (so clearly drawn by Ewing) between entailment and awareness. To say that X entails Y is not to say that I am aware of Y whenever I think of X. Alternatively Maclagan confuses phenomenology with metaphysics and the *ordo cognoscendi* with the *ordo essendi*. Because I am not aware of God when I answer moral claims it does not follow that his existence is not required as their ground.

Secondly, even if we confine ourselves to phenomenology we may well hesitate before accepting Maclagan's dogmatic (and pejoratively coloured) assertion that a theistic view of moral obligation is possible only if the moral consciousness has been vitiated by beliefs acquired by a wholly non-moral route. The assertion is a caricature of Hebrew ethics from which, historically, Maclagan's outlook is derived. The Jews did not first have a secular sense of obligation to which, as a kind of afterthought, they added a 'numinous fringe' engendered by a totally separate 'sense of the divine'. Their morality was conditioned by religious faith throughout their history.[16]

I do not therefore think that Maclagan undermines the argument to God from moral claims. On the contrary he has confirmed it; for his own reasoning has brought us to the frontier of religion; and, once misunderstandings are removed, we have good grounds for an intuitive act of faith.

Lest any misunderstanding should remain—and it is likely that I have sometimes used incautious language in presenting the theistic case—I must stress the following points.

1. Although the believer derives morality from the will of God he need not be aware of the derivation every time he passes a moral judgment or makes a moral choice. In fact he need be aware of it only in special moments (for example when he brings a problem before God in prayer) or when his duties are themselves religious (for example when he resolves to say his prayers even though he may not want to do so).

2. It is again necessary to recall the relative independence of ethics and the distinction between the *ordo essendi* and the *ordo cognoscendi*. Even within the religious life the 'autonomy' of ethics is preserved. Even when a believer consciously identifies an action with God's will he is also simultaneously aware of it as being right in purely moral terms. Indeed he must be antecedently aware of its congruence with the moral law; for otherwise he could not ascribe it to God's will.

Such ethical autonomy is required by the Christian account of divine action both by nature and by grace. God does not act merely from without in discontinuous moments of 'encounter'; he also acts within through the illumination of his Word and

---

[16] C. A. Campbell (in his *Selfhood and Godhood*, London 1957) adopts a position similar to the one held by Maclagan. Having admitted that jurisprudents always define positive law in terms of an imponent he denies that it is necessary to posit God as the author of the moral law. 'It is of the very essence of moral obligation, as we experience it, to be self-sufficient, to carry its authority wholly within itself' (p. 381). '*Per se* the analysis of moral experience yields no more than that there is a moral order rooted in the very nature of reality'. (p. 382). But moral experience need not contain an awareness of the God whom nevertheless it presupposes. Furthermore the affirmation of 'a moral order rooted in the very nature of reality' is the kind of vague metaphysical assertion that justly earns the reproach of logical analysts. I, for one, cannot give it any meaning unless it is theistically interpreted.

Spirit. Having made us in his image he has given us the power to discern the rightness of those actions which are in accordance with his will.

Existentialist theologians do well to stress the transcendence and hiddenness of God; but they often forget (if they do not deny) that God is also immanent; and so they fail to locate his 'hiddenness' in the soul of man. Yet the affirmation of God's hidden presence within all men is necessary if we are to interpret the moral life religiously without obliterating its distinctive nature.

Furthermore, it is only by holding transcendence and immanence in right proportions that we shall be able to understand the double character of the pressure which the moral law exerts. This comes to us from without and bears the stamp of an objective fact. But we also experience it as something which is somehow lodged in our higher, or better, selves where it becomes the governing principle of our being.

We can now answer the question: 'what does the atheist know when he recognizes authoritative duty-claims?' I have already rejected the view that he knows God by an act of 'unconscious faith'. Yet we cannot separate the object of his knowledge from God's activity if God is the ground of the moral order. We can now see that the atheist *immediately* knows the created effects of God within his soul through his conscience which is God's 'voice'. But he cannot trace the mandates of conscience to their true external source. When he attempts to do so he either reduces the source naturalistically (equating it, for example, with the pressure of society) or (detecting its non-natural character) he equates it, as Maclagan does, with an impersonal order of values for which there is no analogy in experience.

3. The identification of moral claims with God's holy will is not free from ambiguity. On the purely moral plane obligation is self-evident; for there is nothing else through which it can be understood. But when it is equated with the will of God it is not immediately self-evident. That God is holy in himself does not require any further explanation; but that he requires his creatures to be holy does require one. It is insufficient to reply that he has a right to command because he made us; for the mere fact that he made us cannot constitute an obligation.

Here we must discard the last shreds of naturalism. Even those who would not otherwise speak naturalistically of God are apt to construe his creative act solely in terms of power. That his creativity manifests a unique mode of power is true; but the power is suffused by love; and it is the love that constitutes the final ground of obligation.

Yet we must not think that God's love is separate from his holiness; for his will reflects his character. His holiness *is* love. He made us out of love in order that we might share in the love that is his very being. Just as his will of love is the imperative of the moral law so also his character of love is the exemplar of the moral life.

4. Therefore, while theism 'explains' obligation it does not 'explain it away'. The constraint of God's will and our corresponding duty to perform it are self-authenticating moral facts. Just as the content of the moral law must always be perceived by Christians and non-Christians equally through the autonomous operations of the conscience even when the content is referred to the character of God, so also the form of the law as an unconditional obligation must be autonomously experienced even when it is referred to God's sovereign will. 'Ought' is always irreducible.

It is surely obvious that here we have the highest case of obligation. Even in our finite lives we know that there is no stronger obligation than one imposed by a friend who has showered his gifts on us with self-less generosity; and that correspondingly there is no stronger duty than a debt of gratitude. Therefore morality, so far from being negated, is fulfilled in the belief that the whole life of duty is a debt of gratitude to God for his great love in creating us to share in his perfection.[17]

5. By faith, then, we identify the form and content of the moral law with God's will and character. God wills us to be truthful and compassionate because he possesses these qualities to an infinite degree. Out of love he created us to share his holi-

---

[17] W. G. De Burgh wrote that 'love precludes all thought of obligation' (*From Morality to Religion*, London 1938, p. 66). This statement, while applicable to Platonic *eros*, is directly contradicted by the New Testament's formulation of Christian *agape* in such terms as 'Thou *shalt* love thy neighbour as thyself' and 'Beloved, if God so loved us, we *ought* to love one another'.

ness; and our duty to fulfil the moral law is our answer to his love.

Yet on occasions it is hard know how claims are to be satisfied. Sometimes they conflict. At other times we are uncertain of the *manner* in which they are best fulfilled. How, then, can we be sure that we are doing God's will? I can here only offer a few, brief, observations.

(a) The Christian is used to the idea that he can never perfectly perform God's will. In this life he remains *simul justus et peccator*. Even when his duty is entirely plain (as it very often is) he knows that he is deficient in his inner attitude if not also in his outward acts. It is therefore not surprising if he exhibits deficiency in those choices which require special insight and imagination.

(b) Yet we can always be sure of doing God's will to some degree so long as we answer claims to the extent that our vision and circumstances here and now permit. Doubtless if we were closer to God our vision would be clearer and our circumstances more propitious. But in every situation we can discover *some* manner of embodying *some* element of the moral law; and so we achieve a degree of approximation to, and co-operation with, God's will.

(c) We must not assume that even in a wholly obedient life God's will is fully known in advance. Even in Gethsemane Jesus hoped that God would spare him crucifixion. Therefore the moral condition even of the saints is often one of *docta ignorantia*. De Caussade stated this painful truth as follows:—

'It is no doubt a great blow, as of death, to the soul, this loss of the sight of the Divine Will which retires before her eyes to take up a position behind her, as it were, and impels her forward, being no longer her clearly conceived object but becoming her invisible principle.'[18]

(d) Therefore in cases of real doubt we cannot invoke the will of God as a *criterion* for moral choice. His will is here a mystery. It cannot become the 'clearly conceived object' that ethical judgment needs. We may *feel* that an action is demanded by

[18] *Self-Abandonment to Divine Providence* (English trans. by A. Thorold, London 1955, p. 110).

God's will for us here and now; but since the feeling can be illusory (as the behaviour of 'enthusiasts' has shown) we are obliged to justify the action on independent moral grounds.

(e) When Christians differ in their attitudes to complex moral problems we need not conclude that the one obeys, and the other disobeys, God's will. Thus in the conditions of our evil world it may be God's will that some Christians should be pacifists and others non-pacifists. It *may* be so. Our ignorance is necessarily complete.

To sum up, we can say that the form of the moral law as a categorical imperative is the personal command of God and that the general precepts of this law constitute the content of his will. But in complex and difficult situations we cannot be sure that we have chosen the course that a *perfect* obedience to his *particular* will for us *here and now* requires. At the same time Christians believe that as they learn to rely on him he will enable them increasingly (often through their very failures) to know and do what is pleasing in his sight. How far we have strayed from his will (both when it is plain and when it seems obscure) is known to him alone; for he alone discerns the thoughts and intents of the heart; and as we fear his judgment so also we trust in his salvation.

My remarks have been inevitably circumscribed. I have considered God's will solely in relation to moral choice. But we dare not forget his universal sovereignty. Since he is King he will defeat the powers of evil and establish his eternal Reign. Therefore we can speak of a 'plan' which he is 'working out' and which he will 'fulfil' at the 'end of history'.

While the great themes of providence and eschatology fall outside the limits of this book there is one point on which the Christian moralist has special reason to insist. Since God's sovereignty is one of love he acts, not by coercing the human will, but by eliciting its free response. Therefore the final enactment of his will cannot be anything other than the completion of our obedience to his law—the perfect law of liberty whereby we become his sons and heirs of everlasting life.

Chapter 4

GOODNESS

IN its most general sense 'good' stands for whatever is the object of approval or desire. This sense is evident in our basic utterances. 'Good!' is our way of endorsing or commending a statement or a situation. Therefore the subjectivists are right in saying that approval (or a cognate attitude) is a necessary condition for the use of 'good'; but they are wrong in saying that it is an ethically sufficient one.

We must further distinguish between (a) moral and non-moral goods, and (b) intrinsic and extrinsic ones. (a) Pleasure, friendship, and artistic creativity are all 'goods' in the sense of being things we desire. But they are not (necessarily) moral goods. (b) An intrinsic good is one we desire for its own sake; an instrumental good is one we desire as a means to something else.

It is also natural to say that we 'value' the things which elicit our approval or desire. Correspondingly we can apply the noun 'value' and the adjective 'valuable' to goods of every kind. We inevitably construct a hierarchy of values. To have a right 'sense of values' is to have a capacity for recognizing their relative importance. Thus many humanists would agree with Christians in maintaining that intrinsic goods are superior to instrumental ones, and that among intrinsic goods moral goodness is supreme.

Finally, 'good' can have a teleological significance. It can stand for that at which any being aims in order to actualize its nature or specific form. On this view anyone can call anything his 'good' if he thinks that it contributes to his self-fulfilment. But this 'good' (even if it is regarded as a supreme good or *Summum Bonum*) need not be morally good or even compatible with morality.

In this chapter I shall deal solely with moral goodness. I shall consider its relation to the teleological sense of good in the next chapter. I suggest that we can see moral goodness as a pointer to God by examining it under three aspects: its evolutionary origin, its status as an ideal, and its relation to empirical fact.

Let us first consider the origin of the moral consciousness. This question could have been raised with reference to moral claims; for the good and the right are complementary aspects of morality. But I have chosen to discuss the question in this chapter rather than the last for two reasons. Firstly, I hope to show that 'good' is ontologically prior to 'right'. Secondly, the same question can be raised concerning the emergence of other values in the cosmic process. The good is traditionally linked with the true and the beautiful. These form a triad of 'intrinsic values'. Hence while I shall refer to claims in order to make my argument cover morality as a whole I have started from the good as the ethical aspect of man's value-consciousness.

One, essentially simple, question faces us. How did man first become aware of moral norms? The failure of naturalism in all its forms shows that ethical terms cannot be reduced to, or explained by, non-ethical ones. Therefore the moral consciousness cannot be reduced to, or explained by, the non-moral state from which it arose. If morality as we now know it is irreducible to non-moral factors its first appearance on the cosmic scene must also be irreducible to its pre-moral matrix.

It is important to note that this problem arises even from a subjectivist account of good and evil; for exponents of subjectivism in its more sophisticated forms concede that there are objective criteria for moral value-judgments and that the moral feelings of approval and disapproval are unique. How, then, did the feelings emerge? We cannot 'explain' them in terms of non-moral criteria and feeling-states without committing the naturalistic fallacy that subjectivists themselves condemn.

The fact is inexplicable unless we make two assumptions. Firstly, the moral order objectively exists as a higher environment to which man can, and if he is to fulfil his essence must, adapt himself. Secondly, the capacity for moral adaptation was instilled and actualized by a designing Power. In order to harmonize these two assumptions we must infer that this Power is the source of the moral order. Furthermore, since impersonal cannot account for personal being we are bound to conclude that this Power is personal as well as holy.

The only alternative 'explanation' open to the atheist is that the moral consciousness was 'latent' or 'potential' in a pre-moral state. But what can this mean? Even if the emergence of mind can be non-theistically understood it is wholly unclear how the mere capacity for the intelligent ordering of desires could even potentially contain the consciousness of moral values; for if naturalism (including evolutionistic naturalism) is false this consciousness is unique.

The words 'latent' and 'potential' are vacuous unless they are related to the creative energies of God. There are two fundamental questions that the atheist cannot answer. How did a non-moral organism acquire a moral potentiality, and how in any case could the potentiality be actualized? The theist answers the first question by affirming that all life possesses its capacities through its relation of *potentia obedientialis* to God's will. The second question is still more pressing. Even if we admit the presence of a moral potentiality we still have to explain how it could be actualized. Here the principle enunciated by Aquinas in his *Prima Via* is self-evident. The potentiality can be actualized only by a being that is in this respect already actual—that is, by the personal Goodness we call God. The same point can be put by saying that the emergence of the higher from the lower is inexplicable unless the higher exists as an eliciting influence.

At this point the atheist sometimes takes refuge in 'Nature' as an explanatory idea. His argument is that nature contains more than we know. With our limited vision we see only a part of nature; but the part we do not see is a dynamic force that runs throughout—an *élan vital* that is capable of producing new (including moral) modes of being.

This theory of nature, when pressed, passes into either theism or absurdity. If nature can produce the sense of a moral order how can it be less than moral itself? Moreover it must be a designing power. But a natural power so defined would be strictly supernatural; it would transcend the concept of nature which is our normal one and from which the argument is bound to start; it would in fact be equivalent (in this context and for this purpose) to what Christians mean by God.

However, even if we are constrained to postulate a supernatural, moral being as the efficient and final cause of the moral sense need we also assume that he is Creator of all things? May he not be, for example, a Platonic Demiurge who fashions moral beings out of pre-existent matter? While a coercive proof is not available there are many reasons for postulating a Creator rather than a Demiurge. The following considerations seem to me to be especially cogent.

Once we begin arguing teleologically it is very hard to stop. The demand for one explanation prompts the demand for another. No sooner have we traced a designing Intelligence at t 6 in the evolutionary process than we are compelled to trace it at t 5 and t 4 as well until we come to the beginning of the process when the teleological passes into the cosmological argument and we see God as the cause of the world not only *in fieri* but also *in esse*.[1]

Thus morality presupposes reason. And the latter, no less than the former, calls for an explanation in terms of a designing Mind. How could reason have been produced from a pre-rational state? It is as useless to 'explain' reason as it is to 'explain' morality by saying that it was previously present in a 'potential' form or that it was generated by an all-inclusive 'Nature'.[2]

Furthermore, we have to proceed from man's mental to his physical constitution. Recent developments in both physiology and psychology have shown how closely body and mind are linked within the human organism. How, on the cosmic scale, can we understand the pre-adaptation of bodily to mental functions unless we postulate a Designer? The only alternative is to ascribe the pre-adaptation to sheer 'chance'; but the odds against the random appearance of a material structure favourable to mind are enormous; so that if we feel compelled to postulate an

---

[1] I hold that the cosmological argument is valid whether or not the world had a temporal beginning. I have introduced the argument in this way in order to show that the more we examine nature's elements the more we are compelled to ask why anything exists at all.

[2] Thus it is no explanation to say, as Julian Huxley does (*Evolution in Action*, p. 93), that 'all living substance has mental, or we had better say mind-like, properties; but these are, for the most part, far below the level of detection'. The non-explanatory nature of this assumption becomes apparent as soon as we admit (as Huxley does on pp. 114-15) that the ability to form symbols and concepts makes the human mind a wholly new phenomenon.

Orderer for mind we shall find it reasonable to postulate one for mind's physical antecedents.

Yet it must be admitted that however far back we trace an Orderer (and there are signs of 'prospective contrivance' in sub-human nature also) we never of logical necessity reach a Maker of *all* things. We may think it is incredible that a Designer who exercises such extensive mastery over his material should not also be the Creator of it. We may think it incredible that he should be able to produce the rational and moral consciousness *de novo* if he did not produce everything *ex nihilo*. We may think these things, but we cannot prove them without grasping the radical *contingentia mundi* which it is the province of the cosmological argument to express. This is as it should be. The proofs converge on each other; but each has its special point.

To return to the strict confines of my subject, unless we suppose that a holy God designed our moral nature we cannot explain its origin. Yet I realize that this argument differs from my other arguments in passing beyond morality itself to its cosmic context and in appealing to the speculative more than to the practical reason. Therefore I do not wish to press it unduly. My chief concern is with the theistic implications of the moral consciousness as it now is. To these I return.

My second argument concerns the *status* of goodness as an *ideal*. I can best introduce the problem by recalling the various senses of objectivity that I gave in chapter one.

I maintained that in ethics the words 'objective' and 'object-ivity' can signify three things: the actual possession of moral properties by human beings, the universality of principles or norms, and the independent existence of moral entities as con-stituents of a spiritual order. I further maintained that, while both claims and values are objective in the first and second of these senses, only claims need be *immediately* regarded as objective in the third. I shall now argue that on reflection we are obliged to ascribe independent existence to values also.

Both the Platonist and the Christian affirm that values exist *per se* in an intelligible realm. Plato held that they exist (or sub-sist) impersonally, as Forms or Ideas, without any personal ground. The Christian regards them as elements in the self-existent personality of God.

73

The Moral Argument for Christian Theism

For the moment I shall not choose between these two accounts. I am concerned now to defend the basic thesis, shared by both, that moral values (as expressions of 'the good') exist independently. Whether they are personal or impersonal is a question I shall examine later. Of course if (as I have argued) claims imply a Claimant, and if the order of claims is the same as the order of values, it will follow that the Christian explanation is the true one. But the identity of the two orders has not yet been shown.

The question, then, that must be answered first is whether we need to infer that moral values exist *per se* in a spiritual realm inaccessible to sense-experience. It seems to me that four reasons can be given for this inference. I shall review each of these, although I consider that only the fourth is valid.

1. The first argument would be along the lines of Aquinas's Fourth Way which runs thus :—[3]

'The fourth argument is taken from the degrees of reality we discover in things. Some are truer and better and nobler than others, so also with other perfections. But more or less are attributed to different things in proportion as they variously approach something which is the maximum. Hence, there is something truest, and best, and noblest, and in consequence the superlative being, for the greatest truths are the greatest beings. Now the maximum in any order is the cause of all the other realities of that order. Therefore there is a real cause of being and goodness and all perfections whatsoever in everything; and this we term God.'

The basis of this proof is that relative degrees of perfection imply the existence of perfection in an absolute degree. The proposition that 'the maximum in any order is the cause of all the other realities of that order' is a further point that need not be discussed; for unless the prior argument from relative to absolute is valid it is irrelevant. The argument's validity can be queried on two grounds.

Firstly, even if we grant the necessity of moral norms it does not follow that they are in the strict sense absolute. They might be no more than very high ideals, as F. R. Tennant pointed out.

[3] *Summa Theologica*, 1a. ii. 3. (translated by Thomas Gilby, *St. Thomas Aquinas : Philosophical Texts*, Oxford 1956, No. 153).

74

'Our moral experience, evaluation, and progress presuppose norms and ideals; but it is no more obvious that they presuppose an absolute, infinite, or perfect norm than that our growth in stature presupposes the existence, or even the idea, of an infinitely tall giant.'[4]

The only possible answer to this criticism is that an existential move from relative to absolute is valid *only* in the case of values. Thus while it would be obviously absurd to argue from varying degrees of height to an absolute form of it we can argue from varying degrees of goodness to its absolute existence. But why should we make values an exception? It is hard to see what reason could be given.

Secondly, even if we were forced to posit an absolute norm of goodness we need not affirm that it exists. It might be no more than a 'regulative idea' or 'limiting concept'. The only way of proving its existence would be to invoke the ontological argument. One wonders how far this argument may have been presupposed unconsciously by those who have found Aquinas's Fourth Way convincing; for while Aquinas himself rejected the argument his Fourth Way is closer than any of his other Ways to Platonic 'essentialism'.

2. It might be suggested that the transition from idea to existence could be made by an ethical application of the Augustinian argument used by Descartes in his *Third Meditation*. In its simplest form the argument runs thus. I have the idea of an absolute and immutable Good; but I am a contingent and mutable being; therefore I could not form the idea unless a corresponding Reality exists and communicates it to me.

This argument has the merit of simplicity and is bound to attract those of a Platonic temperament. Thus it was accepted by Dean Inge. 'Whence,' he asks, 'comes our idea of God, if not from God himself? Who else could have put it there? Since then we certainly have an idea of God, and since only God can have put it into our minds, we may infer that God exists.'[5]

However, we cannot prove it to be impossible that the human mind, perceiving the partial and mutable nature of its own goodness, could (by an act of imagination) postulate the existence of a Goodness that is infinite and immutable. We can of course

---

[4] *Philosophical Theology* (Vol. 2, Cambridge 1930, p. 98).
[5] *Faith and Its Psychology* (London 1910, p. 182).

affirm that finite *existence* implies infinite existence, according to the cosmological argument; but we can subscribe to this argument without holding that it is possible to infer the existence of God from the idea of him.

3. The theist can attempt to prove the existence of a moral Absolute on the ground of religious experience. The core of the argument is that the religious person feels himself to be in the presence of an ineffable, all-encompassing, mystery. Those who practise the 'higher' religions (pre-eminently Judaism and Christianity) interpret this mystery in terms of moral holiness. This experience guarantees the existence of its object.

The argument is invalid. The experience may be psychologically self-authenticating to its possessors; but it is not logically so to the sceptic. All the sceptic needs to do is, firstly, to dispel the numinous element by the usual methods of reductionism, and secondly to show that what is left is a purely moral experience of an absolute (or at any rate very high) ideal which (for the reasons I have given) need not objectively exist. In short it can be said that a numinously toned morality is no more than morality in a primitive and impure form.[6]

Two negative lessons must be drawn from these attempted proofs. Firstly, we cannot prove the existence of a moral Absolute by analysing our ideas. Secondly it is not possible to prove the point by appealing to experiences of a distinctively religious kind. The positive corollary is plain. The argument from values, like the argument from claims, must show how *moral* experience presupposes God's existence as its ground.

4. Moral values affect us under two modes: attraction and obligation. Firstly, they attract us as 'ideals' toward which we 'aspire'. But we are all victims of an inner conflict. On the one hand we are moved by a desire for goodness 'in itself'. On the other hand we are moved by base desires: our greed, ambition, self-esteem. The supreme moral task, from this standpoint, is to cultivate the desire for the good so that it will either

---

[6] Thus if the sceptic reduced Isaiah's vision of Yahweh's holiness to a Kantian reverence for the moral law we could not answer him by repeating that in Isaiah's experience morality and religion were united. We should of course undermine his case if we could show that his reductionist argument was logically fallacious; but even so we could not validate Isaiah's vision except by an independent argument from non-religious premisses.

obliterate or transform the lower desires which in our better moments we despise.

Secondly, values can be viewed in terms of obligation. We feel not only attracted to them by a natural desire, but also obliged to enact them to the greatest possible degree. The difference between obligation and attraction may be illustrated thus. Let us suppose that we are contemplating someone who is conspicuously good. In so far as we feel attracted to him we may say: 'how I *wish* I were like that'. But in so far as he presents a challenge we say: 'how I *ought* to be like that'.

It is a marked deficiency in many moralists that they fail to perceive in values an obligatory as well as an attractive power. The deficiency is understandable in so far as the element of obligation was (to say the least) not prominent in the thought of Plato. But the moral consciousness requires (to put it in historical terms) that we combine the Platonic with the Kantian attitude by viewing values, not simply as ideals that attract a natural desire, but also as facts that impose an unconditional obligation.

Assuming, then, that goodness both obliges and attracts I now wish to ask two questions. Does our experience of goodness compel us to regard it as existing independently? Secondly, if it does so exist is it personal or impersonal?

It seems to me that if we are thinking of goodness as the object of aspiration we are not forced to regard it as existing independently. The ideal could be an imaginary one. Whether it is finite or infinite it does not contain the reason for its existence. We can ascribe such a reason to it (if it is conceived in an infinite form) only by adopting one of the arguments I have rejected. We can, of course, fall back on an 'intuition' that the 'ideal' must also be 'real'; but an intuition is not a proof.

However, when we consider the ideal of goodness under its obligatory aspect we are compelled to regard it as existing independently. We must first distinguish between the duty which we owe to persons and our duty to enact the virtues they exemplify. Our duty towards persons refers to their existence, for it takes no account of the degree to which they have actualized their essence. If they are criminals or imbeciles they still exert an unconditional claim through their relation to the God who made and loves them. But our obligation to imitate them is imposed by their essence—that is, by the moral goodness they embody.

Yet we are obliged, not by the goodness of a person in so far as it is his, but by goodness 'in itself'. This statement is proved by the fact that the imperatival quality of goodness can survive the removal of each finite instance. Let us suppose that we have felt the constraint of goodness by meditating on the life of Socrates. The constraint would not disappear if we found reasons for believing either that he did not possess the virtues ascribed to him or even that he did not exist. The essence of goodness would remain. It, and it alone, would still constrain us.

What status, then, are we to give this essence or ideal? There are two possibilities. Either it is a mere notion which we abstract from particulars or it has an extra-mental (independently real) existence. It seems to me that the first possibility is excluded on one simple ground. An idea (or ideal) cannot possess moral value. Therefore it cannot exert a moral obligation. It would be as absurd to say that the idea of goodness is good as it would be to say that the idea of circularity is circular or that the idea of God is divine.

Yet, it may be objected, do we not speak of being obliged to 'obey' our *vision* of the good and to be 'loyal' to our *ideals* of moral worth? Certainly we do. But what exactly do we mean? We cannot mean that we are constrained by the mental act of envisaging ideals; for the act does not itself embody the ideals of which we speak. We can, of course, say that we experience a distinct duty-claim to produce moral goodness both in ourselves and in other people. But we should then be listing the duty 'to do good' alongside other duty-claims; so that the theist would then justify the inference to God along the lines that I suggested in the previous chapter.

It is vitally important to maintain the distinction between action *sub ratione recti* and action *sub ratione boni*. Both are genuine modes of the moral life; but they must be distinguished for the purpose of ethical analysis. According to the first the claim to enact goodness is one among many claims. According to the second goodness itself exerts a claim. According to the first I say (without further explanation) that I am obliged to be kind and truthful; but I do not derive the obligation from these values; I merely give it as an instance of moral claims in general.

According to the second I say that values themselves impose an obligation; so that 'goodness' and 'claims' are inseparable.

Now, while these standpoints overlap on the question of 'loyalty' to ideals they still remain distinct. From the first standpoint I say simply (without any further explanation): 'I am obliged to pursue the goodness which I see.' From the second standpoint I say: 'The goodness which I see constrains me to follow it with all my powers.' And (as I have said) the ideal could not constrain me if it were merely a notion (a mentally abstracted universal, like whiteness or triangularity). Therefore it must exist *per se* in an intelligible realm.

Once we have established the ontological objectivity of moral goodness on the ground of its obligatory power we can give a new significance to its attractive quality. The mere fact that we aspire to an ideal of goodness does not prove that the ideal exists. But once we have proved its existence on the ground of its constraint we can infer that it is goodness in its independent actuality which attracts us, as a magnet attracts iron filings from afar. Our desire for perfection is not a mere subjective wish. It is our answer to the call of absolute reality.

Yet (it may be asked) do not other (non-moral) values claim our interest and devotion? Surely an artist can be claimed by beauty and a scientist by truth. Admittedly an artist can regard his quest for visual beauty as the expression of a natural desire or as the fulfilment of a particular obligation (for example, the obligation to cultivate one's gifts). But he can also regard the ideal of beauty as something which intrinsically claims his intellectual energies (and perhaps his life).

It seems to me that since beauty and truth exert their own moral claims they too exist *per se*. But I am now concerned with goodness only. I shall examine its relation to truth and beauty in the following chapter.

The second question is whether absolute goodness is personal or impersonal. Are we to equate it with Plato's Idea of the Good or with the personal God of Christianity? The second alternative is preferable on at least two grounds.

In the first place, if on the finite scale moral qualities inhere in persons (and not things) it is natural to infer that they are personal in their absolute existence. The inference is not only natural; it is also necessary. Plato said that the world of becoming 'participates' in the world of being. But how could we, as persons, participate in a goodness that is *im*personal?

An even stronger proof is afforded by the fact that values exert an obligation. Their obligatoriness is inexplicable unless they are personal. Platonic Forms could, perhaps, attract. But how could they impose an obligation? How could we be in-debted to them? Why should the failure to enact them engender guilt? I can betray a person and I know that I deserve the guilt I feel. But I cannot see how I could betray values if they are *im*personal.

Personal theism gives the only explanation by affirming that value-claims inhere in the character and will of God. In rejecting them we do not merely reject an abstract good; we do not merely reject our own 'good' (in the sense of our 'well-being'); we reject the love which God is in his tri-une being.

These, then, are the arguments which I should use to support the view that absolute values inhere in the personality of God. I shall now attempt to answer some objections raised by W. G. Maclagan. Once again he raises all the crucial points.

Maclagan grants the two premises on which my argument is based. He admits that an 'order of values' exists and that it imposes an unconditional obligation. Thus he writes:—

'Platonic idioms, however inadequate in the end, are here almost unavoidable at the beginning. "Mercy" and "Truth", we know, are not names of historical particulars; but neither, in so far as they belong to the language of value, are they names merely of certain aspects or features of these. Nor again are they just ways of referring to the the whole class (whatever "whole" could signify) of those particulars whose possession of these characters is the basis of our classification. Our articulate understanding of what such valuational words mean, and most generally of the word "goodness", may come only by reflection on particular instances. But we *refer* this meaning, as perhaps we should not do with factual abstractions like "redness" or "painfulness", to something other than the instances. We refer it, I should say, to that which, through the imperfect mediation of our thought, is the inexhaustible source and control of our ability to construct the concrete "picture-ideals", whose realization, if and as they are realized, can then be spoken of as good. It is, I suggest, this source and control of our ideal-framing activity that should be described as an "order of values", in distinction from a "set of ideals". Whatever force there may be in recent criticisms of the language of "non-natural qualities" as a way of stating the truth about what we call moral judgment or value judgment, there is I think a yet more fundamental complaint that might be made both against that doctrine and against at least very many of its critics. It could be complained that they concentrate attention too exclusively on formulated ideals and on actual achievements, and are insufficiently concerned with the nature of our power to create ideals; a power in the exercise of which we may, I believe, be justly described, in Shelley's words, as "the hierophants of an unapprehended inspiration". An order of values, I am maintaining, is implied in any genuine and valid exercise of this power; in any exercise of it, that is to say, that, unlike the arbitrary work of fancy, yields designs for living that are not just indifferently contemplated, nor even simply attractive, but are, whether attractive or not, *authoritative* for us.'[7]

Yet Maclagan will not allow a theistic basis to these values. He accepts them as they are—impersonal entities that have no analogy in our experience. But he is left dissatisfied. He concludes:—

'I readily concede that to speak of an order of values is not to carry our thought to a point at which it may complacently rest. The concept is obscure and problematic in the highest degree. It challenges further enquiry which, if fruitful, might alter our language and thought almost beyond recognition—I wish I knew whether and how. But in default of this enquiry, in which I cannot claim to have made any headway myself, it appears to me that we can neither dispense with the concept—it must be taken as having anyhow a provisional validity—nor yet relate values in any helpful way to some other Being supposedly more fundamental. The beginning of wisdom may here lie simply in getting used to the concept of values as a concept of what *is*, though not as temporal existents are. It may no doubt take some getting used to.' (pp. 91-92).

[7] Op. cit. pp. 85-6 (italics his).

Since an independently existing order of values is inexplicable, and since (as Maclagan so candidly concedes) this inexplicability is a philosophical offence, it would seem natural to accept a theistic explanation. Maclagan rejects this explanation in its two forms.

Firstly, the explanation may take the form of regarding God as one who perfectly exemplifies the order of values. 'He will be, so to say, the Great Exemplar, so that the spiritual striving of men could very properly be described as a ὁμοίωσις τῷ θεῷ, a becoming like God so far as we can. But the order of values as such, if it is to be allowed objective reality at all, must still be said to have being, in its own characteristic mode of being, as something other than and apart from him, and it, rather than he, will be the true Deity' (pp. 88-9).

Secondly, the theist may try to integrate God and values by speaking of God as one who *is* goodness; but Maclagan rejects this way also, though less confidently. 'A verbal formula for such integration might be that which speaks of God not as good but as self-existent Goodness, holding that in 'him' essence and existence are one. Although I cannot claim that in my own case any positive understanding attends the use of such language I can admit that one might feel driven to employ it' (p. 89).

There is no need to linger over the first of these explanations. The Christian theist cannot accept the view that God exemplifies an order of values which exists apart from him. While in the order of knowing philosophical reflection may seem to suggest that God gives 'extrinsic backing' to values, in the order of being values have no existence outside his character and will. We have already seen that Maclagan fails to distinguish between the two orders with reference to moral claims. The same failure seems to determine the false dilemma which he states in his first explanation. From the standpoint of *ethical* knowing it is inevitable for us to speak of 'grounding' absolute goodness in divine personality. But in the order of being (and so from the standpoint of *religious* knowing) Goodness and God are identical.

So I come to Maclagan's criticism of the second explanation. The idea of self-existent Goodness, he says, is a 'verbal formula' of which he does not have any 'positive understanding'. But it is obvious that since we cannot know God's essence, our positive concepts of him are in the last resort inadequate. Maclagan, of course, could have taken the extreme empiricist view that these concepts are therefore meaningless; but he is reluctant to do this; and in any case his own theory of subsistent values is a metaphysical offence that is (on his own showing) insurmountable.

It is impossible to offer any irrefragable proof that will enable us to choose between traditional Christian theism and Maclagan's diluted Platonism. Both will be unacceptable to a person who denies that the speculative reason can ascertain truths concerning the nature of a spiritual reality that totally transcends the world of sense-experience. But if speculation is permissible at all I believe (on the grounds I have given) that it leads to the God of Christianity.

The need for a theistic interpretation of morality becomes especially apparent in Maclagan's treatment of the relation between the 'right' and the 'good'. Once again theism would have saved him from philosophical bankruptcy. He formulates the problem thus : —

'On the one hand we have the problem of the absoluteness of the moral demand, its unquestionable authoritativeness. On the other hand we have the problem of the nature of that objective "order of values", belief in whose reality is presupposed in every endeavour to determine correctly the changing content of our duty in the changing circumstances of our lives. It may be that in the end these two problems coalesce; I mean, it may turn out that the only way of understanding the authoritativeness of the demand is to view it as a function of the absolute importance of what is demanded. But if this is true, at least it is not a truth 'of the first look'. On the contrary, it could, I suspect, only be explained in terms of a sort of moral eschatology, for which the various secular concerns that yield the content of our duty are morally urgent, are in fact *duty*, only through their "participation" in and "relevance" to a different and non-secular order. The vital words "participation" and "relevance" here serve merely to signal a perplexity, which I must leave unresolved.' (p. 55).

Maclagan, properly, wishes to satisfy both aspects of the moral life. On the one hand we are aware of claims and obligations which are elements in an objectively existing moral law and which demand fulfilment apart from any good which they exemplify or produce. On the other hand we are forced to postulate objectively existing values which are no less authoritative than particular duty-claims.

Yet Maclagan also wishes to interrelate the right and the good. He does so by subordinating the first to the second. Particular duty-claims are obligatory through their 'participation in' and 'relevance to' values. At the same time he confesses that he cannot define the nature of this participation.

Theism illumines the priority of values over claims (and thereby of the good over the right) in three ways.

(a) The natural law acquires both its meaning and validity from its participation in the eternal law of God. But God cannot command or exert claims on himself. His law in itself is simply the perfect order of his goodness which is one with his existence. Its obligatory nature is relative to a creaturely mode of being.

(b) Furthermore, even creatures would not experience God's law as a command if they were free from sin. If we were sinless we should spontaneously enact his law. Such spontaneity is the aim of Christians here and now; but they will not attain it fully until the life to come. In Paradise claims and our corresponding duties will have passed away.

(c) Therefore when we view actions solely *sub ratione recti*— when we think of them simply as answers to claims which have no immediate reference to value—we view them in a provisional and partial way. Our final reason for performing them is to express in a finite mode the infinite goodness of the Creator.

It is God's goodness—the love which he is in his inmost being —that constrains us. And (according to the 'moral eschatology' of Christian theism) it is for the vision of his goodness 'face to face' that he is preparing us in every claim that he imposes (both *sub ratione recti* and *sub ratione boni*) in our earthly pilgrimage.

A further reason for ascribing a theistic basis to morality is one that has been stated many times by Christian and non-Christian thinkers. Its premiss is the contrast between values and existence.[8] On the one hand we are obliged to obey the moral order

[8] I could have examined the argument of this section in the light of particular duty-claims; and I shall refer to these as well as to the general

unconditionally. On the other hand our achievement of the good is thwarted by the evil powers of sin and death. Our moral natures cannot be fulfilled unless we are destined for another world in which the realm of values can be perfectly expressed.

The agnostic, admittedly, could reply that even if we cannot hope for eternal life we still have a duty to answer moral claims as faithfully as possible. On this score one of the most telling passages known to me occurs towards the end of H. J. Paton's *The Good Will* : —

' "Let us eat and drink for to-morrow we die" is not the inevitable alternative to a morality founded upon a particular religion, or even to a morality founded upon a religion which demands a belief in a personal God and a personal immortality. To say so is special pleading; it is false to the facts of history; it shows a lack of philosophical understanding and a failure to appreciate some of the highest achievements of the human race. It may indeed make some difference whether we regard men as immortal citizens of a divine kingdom or as mere creatures of a day, as sons of God and temples of the Holy Ghost or as the miraculous appearance of something half divine springing up for a few brief centuries out of a mechanical or animal world. On the latter view we need not deny that some men, perhaps not the best, may be tempted to play a little more in the sunshine while they have it, to give freer rein to their animal impulses, to be a little less careful of preserving intact that diviner spirit which is so miraculously theirs. Some men may consider it not altogether reasonable that a finite and temporal spirit should claim, for a fleeting moment, an infinite and eternal good, when time, as they think, will bring to them not only their own ending but the ending of their race, and the destruction of humanity will be the destruction of all spirit and of all value. Such an attitude may indeed be pardoned, but goodness does not cease to be goodness because of the shortness of the time through which it appears. And some men may rather ask themselves how they can best

claim of goodness. But I have chosen to place the argument in this chapter rather than the last for three reasons. Firstly (as I have just shown) goodness takes precedence over rightness in a theistic setting. Secondly, the contrast is normally thought of as being between the 'ideal' and the 'actual', or 'values' and 'existence'. Thirdly, I shall have to touch on the problem of evil; and 'evil' is the opposite to 'good'.

help their brothers in the brief light of sunshine which precedes their eternal night. Religion may be the completion of morality, and may assure us of that victory which we seek in the world, but it cannot make good evil or evil good. It is not less moral to fight for a victory whose issue is in doubt and whose attainment may be forgotten; and in so doing men at least cannot be accused of fighting in order to win any external reward.'[9]

All this is nobly said. Yet I am bound to raise the following queries. Does Paton fully realize the ultimate effect that explicit atheism can have upon morality? He grossly underestimates both the truth-claims and the transforming power of religion when he says that it 'may' make 'some' difference if we consider ourselves to have immortal souls created and redeemed by God. Conversely he underestimates the moral contradiction involved in our mortality when he calls the latter 'not altogether reasonable'. Again, while the attitude he depicts is perhaps tenable by a Stoic sage can we realistically expect it to be held by a person of average character? Lastly, is it an accident that the passage conveys a mood of stark resignation which, while appealing in its way, excludes the joy which is a mark of Christian sanctity?[10]

However, I realize that the moral argument for immortality raises two important questions. Firstly, does it require belief in God? May we not be *by nature* capable of achieving perfection in another world which *by nature* either does or will exist? Secondly, can the argument (taken in itself) be more than hypothetical? *If* the moral order is to be fulfilled we must affirm that an immortal life is possible. But can we prove that the possibility is a fact? I shall attempt to answer these questions after I have developed the argument through the concept of beatitude. Meanwhile I must deal with one other problem.

The preceding argument presupposes the imperfection of the present world. But how can we square the fact of evil with the existence of an omnipotent and holy God? While I do not dis-

[9] London 1927 (pp. 440-1).
[10] Naturally I entirely agree that religion cannot make good evil or evil good, and that we cannot morally hope for an *external* (or extrinsic) reward; but the moral life would be frustrated unless it had an *intrinsic* reward hereafter; and it is solely this frustration that I am now considering.

pute the propriety of the question I doubt whether a satisfactory answer can be given.

It is surely obvious that the *reality* of evil (in both its moral and non-moral forms) cannot be denied, or even attentuated, by any *a priori* dogma of either a philosophical or a religious kind. Thus it is completely unconvincing to assert that things which 'appear' evil are not 'really' so when they are viewed as elements in a cosmic Whole. Evil acts cannot be compared to musical discords which, while ugly in themselves, borrow beauty from their context. A present wrong can never become right, even if it serves a future good.

If, then, evil is real how can it be compatible with belief in God? Let us first consider moral evil or wrongdoing. Some Christian apologists are content to say that its possibility is inherent in the fact of freedom. God gave man the capacity to choose between good and evil. Therefore it was always possible that man should sin.

This view raises a number of further questions. Why did God grant man this freedom? Would it not have been better to create spiritual beings who would inevitably desire the good? Furthermore how could man have ever chosen evil if he was made entirely by a God who is entirely good? Also was there ever a time when a clear, unbiased, choice was available (as the story of Adam and Eve, if taken literally, implies)? Our knowledge of evolution suggests that when man came on the cosmic scene he was already hampered by ill-formed appetites that were bound to distort his moral judgment as soon as it arose. In any case in the historical period man has never been capable of a wholly undetermined choice. According to the doctrine of Original Sin his nature is 'loaded' in the direction of wrongdoing.

The problem of non-moral evil (especially pain) is no less pressing. We cannot 'explain' the suffering of a child who dies from starvation or disease by saying that it is a 'punishment' for sin. But could we not affirm that it is (in some unknown way) a necessary preparation for another life? We may be driven to affirm this by an act of faith; but the affirmation is not morally self-evident; for why must even eternal happiness be bought at the cost of suffering which the sufferer neither deserves nor understands?

I do not think that the problem of evil can be solved by

speculative reasoning. Von Hügel pronounced the last word when he wrote: 'let us quietly and deliberately admit that no man has yet explained the reality of evil—I mean, of course, the fact of genuine evil, especially moral evil, in a world created and sustained by an all-powerful, all-wise, all-good Spirit, by God'.[11]

Evil, therefore, constitutes *prima facie* evidence *against* the existence of an omnipotent and loving God. On the theoretical plane our perplexity remains. But on the practical plane it is overcome by faith in the redemptive power of Christ. If we lack this faith it is, I admit, always possible that the disorder of the world will prevent us from discerning the divine order to which morality, on other grounds, so amply testifies.

[11] *The Reality of God* (London 1931, p. 17).

Chapter 5

BEATITUDE

IN considering the relation between value and fact at the close of the last chapter I argued that morality demands an eternal life as man's final end or goal. I shall now develop this argument through the concept of happiness or beatitude. I hope to show that the pursuit of happiness, no less than the response to value-claims requires the postulation of God and immortality.

Perhaps the best known form of the argument from happiness to God and immortality is the Kantian one.[1] Therefore I shall discuss it briefly at the outset. It is almost alarmingly clear-cut. In this life goodness is not always accompanied by happiness; but it ought to be so; therefore we must postulate another life in which the defect will be remedied. But we must also postulate God, for only he possesses both a goodness and a power that are sufficient to apportion the rewards of virtue and to create the environment in which uninterrupted happiness will be possible.

It is not hard to see at least three serious flaws in this argument. The first (the logical) flaw was incisively exposed by C. D. Broad thus : —

'There are two different senses of "ought", and one of these involves factual possibility whilst the other involves only logical possibility. If I say: "You ought to do so and so", I do imply that you *could* do so and so in some sense which is not merely that there is no logical contradiction in the notion of your doing it. But if I say: "So and so ought to exist", I imply only that it would involve no logical contradiction, and that any being who could bring it about ought to try to do so. But it does not imply that there actually is any such being. Thus Kant is entitled only

[1] *Critique of Practical Reason* (Pt. 1, bk. 2, chap. 2, sect. 5).

to the hypothetical proposition: "If a perfect God existed he would order the course of Nature so that virtue would receive its appropriate reward in happiness." He is not entitled to the categorical conclusion that such a being exists.'[2]

There is a no less grave (though less frequently observed) objection to the argument from a theological point of view. The relation that Kant posits between God and man, being external, cannot satisfy religious needs. Religions in general, and the Christian religion in particular, certainly affirm that God 'rewards those who diligently seek him'.[3] But in their higher moments they also affirm that the reward is nothing less than the contemplation of God himself. 'Blessed are the pure in heart, for they shall see God.'[4] Religion ends, as it begins, in adoration; and adoration can be fulfilled only in the vision of God 'face to face'.

Lastly, the argument has a strange *ethical* inconsistency. The whole of Kant's moral system rests on the two theses that nothing is unconditionally good except the good will, and that the good will is one that subjects itself to duty for duty's sake according to the maxims of the moral law. One would therefore have expected Kant to spurn the very idea of a reward in the form of an externally conditioned happiness. Do not his ethical principles compel one to infer either that the idea of a reward is morally irrelevant or that virtue is its own reward? Just as the divine Rewarder is a religiously unsatisfying *deus ex machina*, so the reward is an ethically unconvincing addendum to the goodness for which it is bestowed.

The first of these objections shows that we cannot argue categorically from happiness to God. I have already conceded this negative point in speaking of the moral demand for a reconciliation between the realm of values and the realm of facts. But even an argument that is in itself, according to the rules of formal logic, only hypothetical can serve an important purpose if it

---

[2] *Five Types of Ethical Theory* (London 1956, pp. 141-2). Whether Kant himself intended his theistic conclusion to be categorical, and if so whether his intention can be reconciled with his rejection of speculative metaphysics in his *Critique of Pure Reason*, are questions which I leave Kantian scholars to determine. I am not sure what Kant meant when he said that the moral argument extends our knowledge 'from a practical point of view'.

[3] Heb. 11. 6.   [4] Mt. 5. 8.

shows that the rejection of the hypothesis renders the moral life self-contradictory.

Furthermore, the conclusion can become categorical if we already believe in God. The argument will then take the form of a deduction from given premisses. The first premiss will be the existence of an omnipotent and loving God; the second premiss will be the present moral state of man; and the conclusion will be that man is destined for an eternal and divinely constituted happiness.

However, I shall take the argument independently (without assuming God's existence on moral or on any other grounds). I therefore do not hope that, as I shall state it, it can be more than hypothetical. But I ask the reader to bear in mind that it can be re-formulated to yield a categorical conclusion if God's existence is presupposed. Hence I have placed it last—after I have given reasons for inferring God from the moral evidence that is fully within our *present* grasp.

However, the second and third objections to the Kantian proof show that we cannot argue even hypothetically from happiness to God unless happiness is interpreted in moral terms and unless it enables us to posit communion with God as our ultimate goal. In other words, our ethics must be teleological from the beginning. Equally the theistic implications of ethics must be *intrinsically* teleological. Therefore we must start with a concept of happiness that is much more profound than the one which Kant offers in his proof. We must integrate the truths of Kantian deontology with the great tradition of teleological ethics that we inherit from Plato and Aristotle, St Augustine and St Thomas Aquinas. The rest of this chapter will be an attempt at such an integration.

The teleological view of ethics rests on three concepts: 'end', 'good' and 'happiness'. While the third is my main theme it cannot be understood apart from the first and second.[5] According to the first, every being moves towards an end or goal that is appropriate to its nature. Man differs from other beings in three respects.

[5] I must stress that in my analysis of these terms I shall deliberately exclude any reference to God. Otherwise my conclusion would be already stated in my premiss.

1. Man alone is aware of the goal (or goals) that he pursues. Leibnitz said that 'nature makes no leaps'. Yet even he regarded self-consciousness as the distinguishing mark of the dominant monads that constitute rational souls or spirits.

2. Man (again unlike the lower animals) is, in his spiritual aspect, free. He can choose between various (sometimes conflicting) ends. He can further direct his actions and even, to some degree, shape his environment in accordance with his choice.

3. The final end of man is obedience to the moral law and value-claims. In an ancient sense of virtue (the sense of the Greek ἀρετή) a being is virtuous to the extent that it actualizes its powers; but these need not be morally virtuous. Yet, while the physical and psychical components of man's nature are not in themselves good or bad they are meant to be harnessed to morally good ends; for only so can he achieve the realization (the ἐντελέχεια) of his specific form.

The concept of 'good' leads to the same conclusion. 'Good' (as I said earlier) can signify the fulfilment of a goal or end. It is that at which any form of being aims. But a man, unlike a plant (and even unlike a dog), does not conform to a pre-determined end. He can choose between different ends. Each of these can become his 'good'—that which fulfils his nature and satisfies his needs.

What then is the *final* good for man? It is moral good. When the question and answer are formulated thus they are free from the naturalistic fallacy. The fallacy would here consist in an *identification* of 'morally' with 'teleologically' good. I am asserting, on the contrary, that we need a prior and distinctive grasp of moral goodness if we are to see that it, and not any other, property is the final good for man.

The same point emerges from a consideration of the view that a virtuous act or habit is one that accords with 'nature'. Those who hold this view do not always make their meaning clear. They are wrong if they mean that a non-ethical analysis of human nature will lead to an understanding either of virtue in itself or of the truth that it is human nature's final end. But they are right if they mean that once we have understood virtue for what it is (a unique form of being with its own imperatival and attractive power) we can *then* see it as our goal.

It is, admittedly, possible to produce empirical evidence in favour of the view that virtue is man's natural 'good' or 'end'. I

Beatitude

have in mind especially the arguments by which Bishop Butler showed that conscience is the supreme principle of human nature. Conscience, he pointed out, distinguishes man from the brutes; its prestige is so strong that even scoundrels pay it lip-service; its neglect produces the gravest disorders in both the individual and society.

Yet Butler also insists, firstly, that conscience proves its natural supremacy by its own intrinsic (or, as Kant would say, 'autonomous') authority; and secondly that its supremacy cannot be grasped unless its authority is *felt*.[6] His empirical arguments are of a secondary, corroborative, kind. Even if they could be weakened by hostile criticism the truth of his moral teleology would remain.

I turn now to my central concept of happiness or beatitude. I shall normally speak of 'happiness' since this is more often used in both philosophical and ordinary speech. Yet 'beatitude' is preferable on many grounds. Having a loftier tone than 'happiness' it suggests that the latter is not to be found in any temporal or sensuous end. Again, in recalling the Beatitudes of Jesus it suggests, more precisely, that true happiness is the spiritual state of those who obey the will of God.

However, I must not anticipate my conclusions. Therefore I shall confine myself to the word 'happiness'. This can have the following senses.

(a) Happiness may mean the 'well-being' of the soul. In this sense it is something that all men desire; but all men do not give it the same content. Aristotle formulates this meaning in his *Nicomachean Ethics*. What, he asks, is the final good for man? 'Verbally,' he replies, 'there is very general agreement; for both the general run of men and people of superior refinement say it is happiness (εὐδαιμονίαν), and identify living well and doing well with happiness (τὸ δὲῦ ςῆν καὶ τὸ εὖ πράττειν ταὐτὸν ὑπολαμβάνουσι τῷ εὐςαιμονεῖν); but with regard to what happiness is they differ, and the many do not give the same account as the wise.'[7]

(b) Happiness can also indicate the activity or object that constitutes well-being, and thereby also the good or end of human nature. Thus if we identify our 'end' with the pursuit of wealth

[6] See especially his second sermon *Upon Human Nature*, sect. 8.
[7] 1095a (trans. by Ross).

93

we can call both the activity of gaining wealth and wealth itself 'happiness'. Similarly if we identify it (as Aristotle did) with contemplation, 'happiness' can be applied both to the act of contemplating and to the object contemplated—to the former directly in so far as it actualizes our intellectual powers and to the latter indirectly in so far as it is the cause of actualization.

In terms of this analysis our final happiness or well-being consists in moral activity. It consists directly in the activity itself; but it can be indirectly referred to the moral order by which the activity is elicited. Admittedly it may seem strange to call the moral order itself one's happiness. Yet it is not so strange if the order is derived from God whom Christians have always found it natural to call their Beatitude and Joy.

3. The third sense is the most familiar one. 'Happiness' can indicate the feelings or emotions that are summed up in the words 'pleasure', 'satisfaction', or 'delight'. I think it is safe to say that whenever we use the word unreflectingly we intend it to bear this sense. Thus in attributing to someone a 'happy' disposition we mean that he by nature *feels* happy even in circumstances that would make most people feel miserable. Similarly in calling experiences happy or unhappy we mean that they cause pleasure or pain.[8]

Whether anyone can consistently aim at pleasure for its own sake is very doubtful. Certainly if anyone did so he would be acting in a way that is incompatible with morality. The moralist is bound to reject even the refined form of hedonism which equates 'the good' with 'the pleasures of a good conscience'. Undoubtedly it is permissible to enjoy those pleasures that our consciences approve. But even then it will, I think, be found

[8] H. J. Paton has shown that Kant contradictorily interprets happiness according to both the first and the third of the above senses. 'Too often —perhaps in order to contrast happiness as sharply as possible with morality—he appears to regard it as little more than the greatest possible amount of continuous uninterrupted pleasure'. But 'Kant combines it inconsistently with another view, according to which we have no determinate and sure concept of happiness as an end which we seek. Here happiness is the total satisfaction of our needs and inclinations' (*In Defence of Reason*, London 1951, pp. 163-4). If Kant had emphasized the second view, clarified it, and related it to Aristotelian teleology he would have seen that the life of duty *is* happiness. The preponderance of the first view in his writings contributes to the formalism that vitiates both his ethics and his theology.

that approval is given to the pleasures because they accompany or follow activities that are desirable on other grounds.

This brief account of human teleology raises many questions. I have selected four.

1. It may be objected that we are not often conscious of choosing ends. Certainly we are not conscious of choosing one final end to which we subordinate all our acts. For the most part we act from habit or routine. We are determined in countless ways by heredity and environment which largely explain both what we are and what we do.

It must be admitted that we do not often choose general ends *explicitly*; but we do so *implicitly* every day. Our particular choices imply the pursuit of universal goods. To put it simply, we all want a few, basic, things out of life; and we all want some of them more than we want others. These things (whether they are freely chosen or determined) constitute implicit ends. Even at a pre-ratiocinative level they are life-goals that shape our characters and move our wills.

Yet sometimes we make a deliberate choice of final ends. Let us take the case of a man who has devoted himself to amassing wealth without fully knowing that this is his dominating aim. It is only when his health suffers or his affections are stirred that he is brought to understand the direction that his life is taking. If he is wise he will see that the pursuit of wealth is bound to corrupt his nature which was made for higher ends. If he reflects further he will also see that his only final end—the only end that can satisfy his whole self—is a life spent in actualizing moral values and answering moral claims.

However, few of us are fully conscious of our goals and few of us integrate them successfully. We so often resemble Plato's 'democratic man'.[9] We pursue contradictory ends—now pleasure, now power, and sometimes (when conscience is unduly pressing) obedience to the moral law. From the standpoint of moral goodness we are neither wholly good nor wholly bad. From the standpoint of the 'good for us' we are torn between love for those temporal things which will feed our empirical selves and love for those eternal values in which our 'true' selves are at home.

2. A second objection is that even if we act for the sake of

[9] *Republic*, 561.

ends we do not always act for the sake of happiness or well-being. It is easy to support this objection by examples. The extreme case is the person who takes his life. Sometimes, moreover, we know that our actions thwart our higher ends. Thus someone may choose drunkenness to drown his sorrows while knowing that it is contrary to the well-being which on other occasions he pursues.

These examples do not disprove the theory. It is still true that we act for the sake of what we *consider* to be our good. The person who kills himself has come to believe that suicide (morally evil though it is objectively) is the only 'good for him'. Equally the drunkard considers (at the moment) alcohol to be his only good—the one answer to his present need, even though he knows that he has other, higher, needs which only self-discipline can satisfy.

We are not, indeed, perpetually aware of our well-being as an end at which we aim. We are usually aware of only those objects and activities by which it is attained. Yet we should not perform any action or aim at any goal unless it fulfilled, if only partially, our well-being. This truth is as applicable to the moral as to any other sphere. An action done from duty may oppose a particular inclination; but it also expresses the final, inner, law of the agent's being; and thereby it is the final means through which he can be happy or 'live well'.[10]

3. It could be objected that in making moral goodness man's chief end I have neglected other values. The morally good is only one member of a triad. There are also the true and the beautiful. Do not these also deserve to be included in man's 'good' or 'end'? Certainly they do; but they are subordinate to moral goodness in two important ways.

Firstly, when we say that beauty or truth exerts a 'claim' on our devotion we mean that it exerts a *moral* claim. Hence we experience guilt if we seek to evade the claim through (for example) laziness or greed. While these values are themselves non-moral they are the objects of distinctively moral attitudes. Furthermore they *can* manifest themselves in moral forms when

[10] Psychologists differ greatly in their descriptions of the human *psyche*; but they agree that in *some* sense self-realization is an inevitable human aim. See, for example, Anthony Storr's *The Integrity of the Personality* (London 1963, pp. 22-30).

they are embodied in a human will. Thus we can be constrained by the 'truthfulness' of a saint and by the 'beauty' of his character.

Again, when the pursuit of truth and beauty conflict with purely moral claims we give priority to the latter. Thus if a scientist neglected his obligations to his family or experimented on persons without their full consent he would be acting in a way that the strongest devotion to truth could never justify. Similarly if we must choose either to preserve a landscape or to use it for building houses which people sorely need (and which cannot be built elsewhere) we cannot doubt that we are obliged to take the second course.[11]

Nevertheless, the conflict between moral and non-moral values is sometimes acute. It can be especially painful in the sphere of art. Thus a person may respond to the beauty of Bach's *St Matthew Passion* without having the least intention to practise the virtues that the crucifixion signified. Conversely a person may be aesthetically a Philistine and morally a saint. Many readers must have seen this conflict in other people, even if they have not felt it in themselves. I shall later suggest that the conflict can be resolved only by belief in a God from whom all values are derived.

4. The most frequent objection is that once we take happiness as an end we can no longer act for the sake of duty. It makes no difference that we interpret happiness, not in the narrow sense of pleasure, but in the wider sense of well-being; for it is still *my* well-being at which I aim; and so I cannot aim at moral goodness 'in itself'.

The following answers can be given to this (admittedly plausible) objection.

(a) If the final end of man is defined in terms of the moral order there cannot be a conflict between happiness and duty. Our happiness *is* our duty. There could be a conflict only if happiness was taken to mean 'pleasure', not 'well-being', and if duty was reduced to 'the pleasure of a good conscience'. It may be easy for the eudaemonist to slip into this refined form of hedonism; but there is no *logical* need to do so; and it is grossly

---

[11] This observation is no more than a comment on Kant's celebrated statement at the beginning of his *Grundlegung* that there is nothing unconditionally good except the good will.

unfair to equate the essence of a theory with its possible distortions.

(b) It is important to give a *psychologically* accurate account of the relation between happiness and duty. We are not to imagine the case of someone who, having searched for happiness in a thoroughly self-centred way, suddenly finds in virtue the answer to his quest. I have already stressed that we cannot regard moral goodness as 'our good' unless we already feel its claims and choose it for its own, distinctive, excellence.

The reason why moralists find difficulty in reconciling devotion to duty with the pursuit of 'well-being' is that while the reconciliation is being continually enacted it cannot be theoretically stated in a convincing way. If we say that we are morally good *because* we desire happiness we misrepresent morality. But if we say that our happiness is a wholly unintended consequence of moral goodness we shall misrepresent our desire for happiness. The facts are that we are conscious both of serving claims and desiring happiness; that the two interact in many subtle ways; and that the interaction, so far from impoverishing, enriches both. Without a prior grasp of the moral order the desire for happiness flounders in self-centredness. Without a reference to well-being devotion to duty becomes oppressive, arid, and inhumane.

(c) One must distinguish between long-term and short-term choices. A person is helped in his moral efforts by the conviction that goodness is his final end. Yet this does not mean that his action here and now is determined by the thought of beatitude; for, as Aquinas put it, 'a man need not be always pre-occupied with his last end, any more than a wayfarer should always be thinking about the end of his journey with every step he takes'.[12] If the Good Samaritan had been an Aristotelian he would not have given εὐδαιμονία as his reason for helping the wounded man. He was moved, not by a desire for his well-being, but by compassion. But it is an error in both logic and psychology to say that because the thought of happiness would be morally inappropriate here it could not be appropriate anywhere.

(d) If morality is our final end it will determine our lesser ends. If it constitutes our supreme well-being its spirit will pervade all the activities that constitute our well-being in non-moral

[12] *Summa Theologica*, 1a—2ae. i. 6, ad 3 (trans. by Gilby, *Philosophical Texts*, no. 708).

ways. Once again Aquinas expressed the point succinctly. 'Righteousness of heart is required antecedently and concomitantly. None can reach happiness without good will, and the loves of one who sees God inevitably fall in with the divine plan.'[13]

There are several ways of proceeding from happiness to God. I shall take an indirect route. It seems to me that from the philosophical point of view one must first postulate immortality. This is not the order imposed by revelation. On the contrary in the life of faith God (as he is revealed in Christ) is the beginning and the end. Everything else (including the hope of immortality) flows from him as its centre and its source. The order I am following is imposed by natural, not revealed, theology.

If, then, starting from non-religious premisses we take morality to be man's final end, it is not hard to see how at two crucial points the end cannot be achieved within the limits of this present life.

The first point arises from the lasting imperfection of our nature. Nothing less than perfection is our final end. This end is not merely something we desire; it is an absolute obligation. At an elementary stage it may seem enough to discharge the duties of our station in an external form that will satisfy the requirements of society. But when we consider the more stringent claims on our purity of will—claims demanding an *inner* accord with the moral law—we realize how far we constantly fall short.

It is not necessary to support these statements by the doctrine of Original Sin. It is necessary only to observe and introspect. The fact of moral failure is as universally verifiable as any spiritual fact can be. No one admitted it more strongly than Kant. And he could not be accused of subservience to dogma.[14]

If, then, we are to achieve our end there must be another life in which the achievement will be somehow possible. I say 'some-

[13] *Summa Theologica*, 1a—2ae, iv. 4 (trans. by Gilby, op. cit., no. 749).
[14] I am not sure whether Maclagan would assent to the doctrine of Original Sin (even in a modified form). But he affirms all that the doctrine requires from the standpoint of philosophical analysis. Thus he admits that 'history and personal experience suggest, though they cannot demonstrate, the inability of the will even to achieve its own perfection', that 'we must acknowledge that we are in some sort "polluted"', and that 'the will cannot itself cleanse the man' (op. cit. pp. 129 and 130).

how' since I do not wish to prejudge the answer to the question of the means by which beatification will occur. For the moment I wish solely to affirm that unless we postulate immortality we shall have to admit that the individual end of man cannot be fulfilled.

The demand for immortality becomes still more urgent when we reflect on the *social* nature of the moral life. While some duties do not involve any reference to other people, most of them directly or indirectly do so. Hence the chief commandment (on the merely human plane) is to love one's neighbour as oneself. This love (or good-will) is universal in its range. But it takes a special form in the context of our relation with those people to whom we are already bound by natural affection. There is surely no greater human source of true beatitude than a friendship governed by the law of charity.

Now if our final end consists in the personal relationships that we form through love it cannot be reached in this present life. There is no need to argue a point that the deepest experiences of the heart so amply and so painfully confirm. We have only to think of someone whom we loved and who is no longer with us in the flesh. In thinking of him we remember, not only the love we showed, but also the love we failed to show. The failure will stand for ever, as a final frustration of his existence no less than ours, unless we can hope for a perfect state in which our mutual love will be fulfilled.

Yet, even though these moral facts require another life, why should it be an *endless* life? Would not man's end be reached in a life of limited duration? The answer is that a temporally finite life would still be morally incomplete. It would be infinitely less than the eternal end that we could imagine, so that we should lack final happiness. Our misery would be greater, not less, than it is now; for we should have more to lose and keener spirits with which to feel the loss.

However, even if these moral arguments for immortality are sound we must still justify the further inference to God. Christian theism affirms that man's last end (moral goodness) is a participation in the absolute goodness (the holiness) of God. I shall suggest four ways in which this affirmation is required by moral teleology.

1. It is well known that Kant argued from holiness to im-

mortality; but he did not see that his argument also requires the postulation of an infinitely personal God. Having said that the aim of the moral life is perfect obedience to the moral law he continues: —

'Now, the perfect accordance of the will with the moral law is *holiness*, a perfection of which no rational being is capable at any moment of his existence. Since, nevertheless, it is required as practically necessary, it can only be found in a *progress in infinitum* towards that perfect accordance. Now, this endless progress is only possible on the supposition of an *endless* duration of the *existence* and personality of the same rational being (which is called the immortality of the soul).'[15]

The contradiction here is obvious. On the one hand, Kant postulates immortality for the achievement of perfection. On the other hand, in speaking of '*progress in infinitum*' he implies that perfection will always evade our grasp. It seems to me that on the plane of morality the contradiction is inevitable. In this life we cannot imagine goodness apart from evil. Even those whom the Church regards officially as saints are assaulted by sin until the end. Having subdued the passions of the flesh they still struggle with spiritual temptations.

Yet it is not merely a deficiency in imagination that compels us to regard our future moral progress as unending. Human virtue, as we know it, is *objectively* inseparable from temptation. If the threat of sin did not exist our characters would stagnate; and stagnation would be our last, irremediable, infirmity.

This difficulty is at once removed if we suppose that our sinless life in a future world will occur through participation in the holiness of God. We cannot hope to embody God's absolute perfection. But we shall reflect it, as a mirror reflects the sun. God cannot communicate to us the identity of essence and existence that is his alone; but he can and will impart to our perfected natures a living likeness of his immutability. And he will impart it to the extent that we acknowledge in him the source of all the good which, in our earthly pilgrimage, we have

[15] *Critique of Practical Reason*, Pt. 1, bk. 2, chap. 2, sect. 4. (trans. by Abbott, London 1898, pp. 218-9).

sought or won.[16]

2. In any case could a merely human perfection satisfy our desires and so become our last beatitude? We should still be limited, finite, beings. Our resources, even when fulfilled, would not be inexhaustible. Yet they would need to be so if they were to nourish us for eternity.

Consequently, even if merely human goodness could survive without evils to be overcome, we should still be tormented by desire for a higher, an infinite—goodness we could never reach. The torment would be stronger than any we experience on earth; for, having achieved perfection in a finite mode, we should be closer to (and so have a livelier desire for) a goodness that is free from every finite limitation.

These reflections become especially cogent when we consider the life of mutual love that perfected souls would lead. Even within human limits such a life, exceeding all that we at present understand, would be more desirable than any other finite end. Yet it would still not be the greatest end we could conceive; for it would still be less than a common life that is unified and enriched by God.

3. The theistic postulate resolves two perplexities that I mentioned earlier.

(a) I drew attention to the fact that the demands of goodness

---

[16] I fully agree with A. E. Taylor's claim that goodness is not *essentially* inseparable from the evil to which it is opposed (*The Faith of a Moralist*, Vol. 1). He convincingly shows (by analogy with science and art) that in heaven we could progress 'in', though no longer 'to', perfection. But he insists that this progress *in* fruition (which he rightly regards as the transfiguration, not the abolition, of morality) will be possible only if we share in the unchanging perfection of God. Even in a sinless state 'there would still be something to be lived for, the completer assimilation of the activities of the human spirit to those of the divine, the practice of adoration, humility and the reception of the grace of God' (p. 407). Again, 'even in a life where there was direct vision of God, we can readily understand that no vision could ever be complete, just because the object of vision is infinitely rich' (p. 410). Finally, Taylor asserts that this progress 'in' perfection will involve a created participation in the *Totum Simul* of divine existence. 'In virtue of the principle that we become like what we behold, a soul in actual vision of God is assured that it cannot forfeit that vision, for he who *sees* the good can desire nothing else. But there is always also the awareness that there is more to be seen than the soul has yet taken in, and thus the mind's attitude does not cease to be forward-reaching' (p. 432).

sometimes conflict with those of truth and beauty. We may feel that these values are somehow ultimately one. Yet within the limits of earthly life we cannot always do equal justice to their claims. In a narrow sense of morality we find a solution by observing moral claims in preference to non-moral ones. But in a wider sense of morality the solution is incomplete; for we are morally obliged to pursue truth and beauty to the extent that our gifts allow.

If we assume that in a future life our different faculties will be endlessly exercised on purely finite objects it is hard to see how our pursuit of values could be unified. Even if we suppose an enlargement of our present powers we still have to envisage a continuation of the diversity that now exists. But in that case would not the present conflict between value-claims break out afresh?

According to the Christian hope the various activities of the human spirit will be united in the contemplative praise of God who combines goodness, truth and beauty in the simplicity of his being. We cannot now understand either the simplicity of God or the unity of a life that is governed by the vision of him 'face to face'. But we have a foretaste in the spiritual beauty and wisdom of his saints.

(b) If we assume that the object of our beatitude is a God of love we can give a new answer to the objection that the pursuit of our own well-being is irreconcilable with the pursuit of moral goodness for its own sake. If God made us to seek our happiness in him we cannot honour him by setting our happiness at nought. E. L. Mascall has stated this truth with admirable simplicity. Having mentioned Peter Abelard's claim (and St. Bernard's denial) that our love for God can be 'disinterested', he writes:—

'At first sight there might seem to be something highly creditable about such an entirely unselfregarding devotion to the God who is supremely worthy of love, but there are two grave objections to it. The first is that the end which God desires above all else for us is that we may achieve complete and permanent beatitude through union with Him, and that it is therefore, to say the least, perverse of us to claim that full-hearted devotion to Him involves indifference to something that He wills. And the second objection is that, since every being that God has made tends naturally to its own perfection, such an attempt is not merely immortal but also pathological. It can lead to such an appalling case as that which is recorded by Mgr. R. A. Knox, of the young priest who, under quietist influence, prayed on his death-bed that God would send him to hell, so that the divine justice and glory might be more fully manifested. The truth surely is that there is nothing sinful in wishing to achieve beatitude, but only in trying to achieve it otherwise than as God has willed. It should surely be a matter for thanksgiving, not for regret, that the one object which can give us full and incorruptible satisfaction is the one object which above all others God has commanded us to seek, namely Himself.'[17]

The same truth applies to happiness in its secondary sense of pleasure or delight. Throughout the ages Christian writers have held out the hope of a heavenly joy that awaits 'those who endure until the end'. If we reject this joy we do not only frustrate our nature which is made to rejoice in its well-being. We also despise God's gift and so contravene his will. Our rejection stems from a Stoic, not a Christian, attitude. Whereas the Stoic regarded virtue as a passionless state of rational self-sufficiency, the Christian regards it as the surrender of the total self to God's joy-giving love.

4. The final ground for postulating God as our beatitude is that if (as I earlier maintained) we are prevented by an inherent weakness from reaching perfection now we shall be similarly prevented from reaching it hereafter. In an endless life our natures would be endlessly imperfect. The struggle with evil would become a Sisyphean task and extinction would be our sole (but unobtainable) beatitude.

The only non-theistic solution of this dilemma is to suppose that man has a *latent* capacity to achieve perfection. Humanists have often claimed that with greater knowledge in an ideal environment our moral blemishes would disappear. Admittedly the claim is so far unfulfilled. But may we not hope for its fulfilment in another life?

It is enough to answer that we cannot speak intelligibly about the future except by analogy with the present. But our present life does not support the view that increased knowledge and an

[17] *Grace and Glory*, (London 1961, pp. 53-4).

improved environment inevitably foster virtue. Why, then, should we hope that, if they are to be merely human, they will confer perfection in eternity? We can hope that they will do so only if they are to be divine—if the knowledge is to be the vision of God and the environment the company of his saints.

These, then, are some of the ways in which it is possible to argue from happiness to God. Yet each way is exposed to the query that I raised with reference to the fulfilment of absolute values in finite existence. We may desire such a fulfilment; but how do we know that it will occur? Similarly we may believe that our well-being can be achieved only in an eternal life with God; but how do we know that the belief is true?

It is tempting to dismiss the belief as a fantasy or 'wish-fulfilment'. On my own admission the Kantian argument, while proving that *if* God exists he will reward those who obey his law, does not prove that he does exist. Even if my argument has a firmer basis in its initial equation of happiness with virtue, is its theistic conclusion any more secure? Do we not have to admit here too that *if* God exists he will be our beatifying end, but that moral teleology cannot prove he does exist?

Certainly the argument from happiness, if taken in itself, is only hypothetical. But if we reject it we must face the following contradictions.[18]

Firstly, the denial of God and immortality makes man the exception to a cosmic rule. Lower forms of being achieve their temporal ends. Man alone desires an eternal end; but this is unattainable. The highest species is the only one whose *nisus* is frustrated. Such a frustration, while not inconceivable, would be incongruous with the 'scientific humanism' professed by many atheists. It would be incongruous with science in so far as it would discontinue the evolutionary process whereby organisms actualize their potential forms through adaptation to their environment; for man would be the only organism that is not

[18] Even if the theistic postulate is a 'projection' or 'wish-fantasy' it is not the product of a *private* or *irrational* desire. The desire is for a *rational* explanation of human life *as a whole*. This contrast was stressed by Henry Sidgwick. The vindication of the moral order in a future state of happiness is 'an hypothesis logically necessary to avoid a fundamental contradiction in one chief department of our thought'. (*The Methods of Ethics*, London 1884, p. 505).

given an environment appropriate to its latent powers. The incongruity with humanism is even more evident. If our immortal longings are deceitful our grandeur is itself our misery.

The second contradiction is a purely moral one. Both the exponents and the critics of ethical teleology are apt to ignore the element of obligation it entails. We do not only desire perfection. We are morally obliged to seek it. Therefore unless there is another life the obligation will be unfulfilled.

One point of logic must be readily conceded. There is no *formal* contradiction in saying both that we are obliged to pursue a goal and that we shall not attain it. A student may be obliged to aim at a standard of scholarship which he knows he will never reach. We often need an unattainable ideal to help us in attaining the goals that lie within our power.

However, this analogy, though relevant to limited phases of the moral life, ultimately fails. The student is obliged to do no more than *strive* for scholarly perfection. When he has reached the level that his gifts allow his obligation ceases. But moral obligation in itself will never cease. We are obliged to seek, not merely the better, but the best—and to seek it to the end. But if the end is death 'I ought' will not, in the last resort, imply 'I can'.

Yet have I not assumed too readily that the moral law requires perfection? Kant has been criticized for making this assumption. Thus Körner writes that the categorical imperative 'does not command the achievement of holiness or "the complete adequacy of the will to the moral law" '.[19]

It is, of course, true that we need not be perfect in order to discharge *limited* obligations of an *external* kind. Thus a highly imperfect person can possess sufficient honesty to return a book lent to him many years before, even if to do so goes against his wishes. Having returned it he has done his duty to the satisfaction of himself, the lender, and the moral law.

However, those commands that involve an inner attitude require that 'complete adequacy of the will to the moral law' which is holiness or sanctity. The supreme example is the command to love one's neighbour as oneself. Undoubtedly it is possible (in defiance of the gospels) to reduce love to a set of manageable rules. But if our neighbour exerts an unconditional

[19] *Kant* (London 1955, p. 166).

claim we are obliged to love him with the perfect disposition that St Paul describes.[20]

Here we must leave the theistic argument from happiness. Perhaps in itself it can do no more than incline the intellect to faith. If it does this much—or even if it merely awakens a dormant sense of 'belonging' to 'another' world—it will have served as a prelude to the Gospel.

[20] 1 Cor. 13. I do not deny that in many situations it is possible to distinguish between a 'minimal' and a 'perfect' obligation. But I should strenuously affirm that the second *is* an obligation (as the New Testament makes clear when it puts its moral teaching into the form of commands, thus showing that the life of 'grace' is the fulfilling, not the negation, of the 'law'). Especially it seems to me undeniable that we do not consider ourselves to have done our duty towards those we love —and we are bidden to love *all* men—until our desire for their wellbeing is pure and complete.

Chapter 6

CHRISTIAN REVELATION

IN the previous chapters I considered various ways in which morality indicates the existence of an infinite, personal, and holy God. While these indications do not constitute objectively coercive proofs they show that only Christian theism can answer fundamental questions that an analysis of the moral life is bound to raise. If, therefore, we are thinking of reason in its discursive sense we can say that on ethical grounds alone theism is reasonable.

At the same time, since discursive reason (*ratio*) cannot provide a deductive demonstration, an act of intuition (*intellectus*) is ultimately required. Whether this act can be produced by the moral argument (either in itself or when taken with other arguments) is a question that cannot be settled by the application of any rules. Any argument *can* awaken faith; but no argument is logically (or spiritually) *bound* to do so.

At any rate it is clear that the knowledge we have of God by reason (even though it may be accompanied by a vivid sense of his reality) is only an obscure reflection of the light conveyed by Christian revelation. This is not surprising. If our concept of God as the self-existent Creator is derived from the Bible we shall expect the latter to specify and confirm the arguments of natural theology.

In this chapter I hope to show how the content of Biblical revelation fulfils the evidence for faith that is obtainable from moral premisses. Our natural knowledge of God is implanted in us by the creative Word who 'enlightens every man'.[1] Yet this knowledge is only a foreshadowing of the supernatural illumination that God gives us in the Word made flesh.

[1] Jn. 1. 9.

If we take revelation to mean, generally, an 'unveiling' of God's nature we must admit that he has revealed himself in many modes and degrees. But Christians maintain that the Biblical form of revelation differs from other forms in the following respects.

1. It is given through historical events. The data through which God reveals himself to the natural reason are of a general kind. Thus it does not matter which person or act we choose in order to show the theistic implications of morality. Again, the cosmological argument can be based on any instance of contingency. Even the proof from religious 'experience' is bound to consider experiences generically.

However, Biblical revelation is mediated through particular events: the Exodus, the Exile, the ministry of Jesus, the life of the apostolic church. These constitute *Heilsgeschichte*—a series of unique occurrences in which the saving action of God takes place. Christianity cannot be detached from these occurrences and reduced to a set of general truths. Both its theology and its ethics are inseparable from their historical origins.

2. Correlatively, Biblical revelation is inseparable from the community to and through which it was given. Under the old covenant God revealed himself to his chosen people Israel. Under the new covenant he revealed (and still reveals) himself through his new Israel, the Church. Certainly in the Bible he reveals himself with special power to selected persons (such as the prophets and St Paul); but their status and message is always conditioned by the life of the 'divine community'.

Here again we see a difference between Christian and general revelation. The latter does not presuppose a communal setting. On the contrary it is often in moments of isolation that the non-Christian (or the Christian when he is acting on the plane of nature) comes to know God. All the arguments I previously discussed can be verified by each person from his own experience. He need not share, or even consult, the experiences of others in order to draw a theistic conclusion from his moral life.

3. Lastly, the Bible records a *full* and *final* revelation. The arguments of natural theology point to God as First Cause, Designer, and Moral Ground. They also suggest that God is personal. The moral argument goes farther than the others in requiring a God of love who will remedy our weakness and

grant us the beatitude of life with him for ever. Yet however much the moral argument may require an omnipotent God of love it cannot reveal him with the fulness and finality that we need for our salvation.

The only full and final revelation is given in Christ who is God manifest in human form. 'No one has ever seen God; the only Son, who is in the bosom of the Father, he has made him known.'[2] 'In many and various ways God spoke of old to our fathers by the prophets; but in these last days he has spoken to us by a Son, whom he appointed the heir of all things, through whom also he created the world. He reflects the glory of God and bears the very stamp of his nature, upholding the universe by his word of power.'[3]

Christ both clarifies and completes the revelation given to Israel. Even the Old Testament speaks of God as one who is infinite in holiness and love. But it also speaks of him as one who is capable of hatred, vindictiveness, and jealousy. This ambivalence disappears as soon as we identify him with the Father of Jesus Christ. In Christ we see that God *is* love[4]—the love that died and rose again on our behalf.

It is impossible to understand the *ultimate* and *distinctive* meaning of Biblical ethics outside this context of revelation. The qualificatory words 'ultimate' and 'distinctive' are important. The Bible admittedly contains many ethical principles and precepts which do not have a directly religious reference. Yet even these acquire a new and final meaning when they are referred to the revelation of which they are a part.

I have already outlined the manner in which the Bible places ethics in a religious setting. According to the Old Testament the law (*torah*) is more than a statutory enactment or even a purely ethical imperative; it is the teaching or instruction given by Yahweh to his people—his 'way' in which they are to walk, and so the means whereby they can share his holiness. Equally the moral message of the prophets is not the product of a merely human wisdom; it is a word sent by God for judgment and salvation.

The New Testament fulfils the Old. Just as the Old Testament derives morality from the revelation of God in the law, so the New Testament derives it from his final, complete, revelation in

[2] Jn. 1. 18.　　　[3] Heb. 1. 1-3.　　　[4] 1 Jn. 4. 8.

Christ. Two passages will serve as illustrations.[5]

It would be generally agreed that Jesus' command to love one's enemies is characteristic of his message. Yet this command is not a piece of pure ethics; it is not based on a self-contained moral intuition. The motive is religious. 'Love your enemies,' Jesus says, 'so that you may be sons of your Father who is in heaven; for he makes his sun rise on the evil and on the good, and sends rain on the just and on the unjust.'[6] Jesus exhorts his disciples to love their enemies, not because it is intrinsically right (though doubtless it is) nor because it is a means of overcoming enmity (though doubtless in some cases it is this as well), but because such love is shown by God who freely bestows his gifts on all.

The dependence of ethics on religion is equally evident in the epistles. Both the content and the inspiration of the moral life are provided by the saving ministry of Christ.[7] The best example is Romans 12.

The epistle to the Romans has a clearly defined structure. Chapters 1-11 deal with theology, and chapters 12-15 with ethics. Paul begins his ethical section thus. 'I appeal to you therefore, brethren, by the mercies of God, to present your bodies as a living sacrifice, holy and acceptable to God, which is your spiritual worship' (12.1). The crucial word is 'therefore'. The ensuing moral precepts are a deduction from the theology of the previous chapters. Christ, so these chapters have affirmed, died and rose again to save mankind from sin : therefore Christians must perform good works as a thank-offering for what Christ has done.[8]

However, while Christian morality gains its ultimate and distinctive meaning through its dependence on Christian revelation

[5] For the dependence of ethics on revelation within the New Testament as a whole see C. H. Dodd's *Gospel and Law* (Cambridge 1951); and for the teaching of Jesus in particular see J. Jeremias' study, *The Sermon on the Mount* (London 1961).

[6] Mt. 5. 44-5.

[7] This would be technically expressed by saying that the epistles deduce *didache* (ethical instruction) from the *kerygma* (the message of the salvation offered through Christ).

[8] 'Therefore' in 1 Pet. 1. 13 has the same point. The good conduct of Christians is a response to the divine mercy by which they have been 'born anew to a living hope through the resurrection of Jesus Christ from the dead' (1. 3).

(that is, on the ministry of Christ) it always has *some* meaning on a non-religious plane. This is evident even in the verses which I quoted from Matthew 5 and Romans 12. It is even more evident in those passages that lack an overtly religious reference or tone.

The task of the theologian is to show how a purely moral interpretation of the New Testament can be transformed into religious faith. The transformation is not continuous. No less than in the arguments of natural theology there is a 'gap' to be crossed, a 'leap' to be made. But, again as in the arguments of natural theology, the act of faith provides a deeper understanding of the ethical data that form its starting-point.

Let us take as an example the supreme moral principle of Christianity—love. Largely through the influence of Nygren it has become fashionable to say that while some types of love—natural affection (στοργή), sexual passion (ἔρως), friendship (φιλία)—are within the unbeliever's grasp, the love which the New Testament describes (ἀγάπη) is something he can never practise, or even understand; for it is derived from the supernatural love of God revealed in Christ.

Yet, while *agape* acquires its ultimate and distinctive meaning from revelation, it can be partially understood and practised by the unbeliever. The proof is given by the parable of the Good Samaritan. We can describe the neighbourly love that the parable illustrates in various ways. We can call it active compassion, practical care, objectively determined sympathy. No definition does justice to the fact. But it is clear that something of the fact can be experienced even by agnostics. Indeed they frequently show a tenderness, generosity, and self-sacrifice that are lacking in many orthodox believers.

The Christian ought never to deny or disparage the love exhibited by unbelievers.[9] Rather he ought to show how it is

[9] Even liberal and humane writers fall into this disparagement. Thus Helen Oppenheimer writes, in the course of an illuminating study entitled *Law and Love* (London 1962), that while a non-Christian can be 'just by rule' or 'kind by nature' he cannot possess what the Christian means by charity. Surely this is an over-simplification. To *some* degree the non-Christian can share all the Christian's moral attitudes. For both of them love is an obligation to perform acts and cultive a disposition which transcend bare justice and yet are to be distinguished from natural benevolence. That non-Christians do in fact fulfil this obligation up to a point is indisputable.

deepened and strengthened by the revelation of God in Christ. On the basis of the gospels and epistles he will unfold the following sequence: the ideal of love that the Good Samaritan represents—the perfect exemplification of this love in the life and death of Jesus—the divine love for man which Jesus embodied —the mutual love which constitutes the eternal life of the tri-une Godhead and which was historically revealed in the love uniting the Father and the Son.

Each item in this sequence is a link in a chain that binds man to God, earth to heaven, time to eternity. Yet while the chain is indissoluble in the *ordo essendi* it is not initially so for the agnostic within the *ordo cognoscendi*. Even when he has been fully shown the historical basis of the chain he may still withhold the act of faith.

Once again it must be stressed that faith can never be coerced by means of formal logic. In assessing the religious bearing of historical facts (even when they are facts of *Heilsgeschichte*) we can expect only an *in*formal logic of the kind that Newman described in his *Grammar of Assent*. The theologian can set out the evidence in the stages I have summarized; but he cannot devise a technique for ensuring that its meaning will be grasped.

However, two difficulties face those who wish to retain Christian ethics after they have rejected Christian faith.

Firstly, in the New Testament the dependence of morality on revelation is sometimes so pervasive that if the reference to revelation is removed the meaning of the text evaporates. Thus if (as the author of 1 John affirms) our love for each other is based on God's prior love for us, what meaning can remain in human love if the reality of divine love is denied? Again, how shall we understand the 'humility' commended by St Paul in Philippians 2 unless we believe in its exemplar? How, too, shall we interpret Jesus' teaching on 'self-denial' and 'service'[10] if we reject his own interpretation of them through his messianic ministry?[11]

The second difficulty is still more serious. According to many

[10] Mk. 8. 34; 10. 41-5.

[11] I do not wish to imply that the unbeliever cannot give *any* meaning to these texts; for I should then be contradicting what I have already said; but he certainly cannot give them the meaning that was originally intended. Yet these are among the texts that appeal most vividly to the moral imagination.

atheists, Jesus and St Paul were as right in moral matters as they were wrong in religious ones. There is, I admit, no logical contradiction here. We sometimes hold true opinions on false grounds. But we do not habitually do so. Yet we are asked to believe that Jesus held ethical views which are wholly true on theistic grounds which are wholly false. The *psychological* contradiction is incredible.

If, then, we take the New Testament *in itself* we find that its moral teaching can both positively and negatively lead the mind to belief in God. I shall now attempt to show how it both corroborates and fulfils the purely rational arguments that I offered in the preceding chapters.

In considering the ways in which Christianity fulfils the moral argument I shall begin with Goodness and then proceed to Duty and Beatitude. In a religious context goodness takes priority in so far as the ultimate aim of the believer is to imitate and share in the self-existent Goodness which is God.

This aim, which is implied throughout the Bible, is explicitly stated by the author of 1 Peter thus: 'As obedient children do not be conformed to the passions of your former ignorance, but as he who called you is holy, be holy yourselves in all your conduct; since it is written, "You shall be holy, for I am holy".'[12] Similarly Jesus summed up his teaching on love, by saying: 'You, therefore, must be perfect, as your heavenly Father is perfect.'[13]

Yet these texts in themselves could be taken as a re-publication of the Mosaic law. The Gospel is distinguished by its command to imitate God *as he is revealed in Christ*. Divine goodness is no longer a transcendent and barely accessible ideal; it has become Man in Jesus; so that both its obligatory and its attractive aspects are identical with his influence.

As one who was both God and Man Jesus offered an example of supernatural perfection. To be his disciple is to follow him. And to follow him is to imitate the qualities of his divine humanity—the qualities of obedience,[14] gentleness,[15] love,[16] endurance,[17] humility.[18] He became what we are in order that we might become what he is.

Christian ethics, therefore, are radically personal. They are

---

[12] 1 Pet. 1. 14-16.   [13] Mt. 5. 48.   [14] Heb. 5. 6-10.
[15] 2. Cor. 10. 1.   [16] Jn. 13. 34.   [17] 1 Pet. 2. 19-21.   [18] Jn. 13. 14-15.

grounded in the person of Christ, the only Son of God. The precepts of Christ, even when taken alone, stand in solitary eminence—if not always for the originality of their content at least for the beauty of their form; but in the New Testament they are inseparable from the person of Jesus himself. The teaching of the Sermon on the Mount would be intrinsically valid if Jesus had never lived; but in fact it derives its significance and power from its exemplification in his ministry.

The distinctiveness of Christian ethics on this score is indisputable. Even the Old Testament does not contain a parallel. The prophets received the Word of God through their personal response both to their own experiences and to those of the nation Israel. But they did not embody the Word any more than Moses, who alone had spoken with God 'face to face', embodied the law. While Hosea could regard his fidelity to the faithless Gomer as a parable of God's love, he could not see in himself, as the apostles saw in Christ, this love's definitive enactment.

Nor in later Judaism did anyone point to a Rabbi as the perfect expression of the law. In the course of an excellent essay the Rabbinic expert Herbert Loewe wrote thus. 'Pharisaism is a religion of ideals; Christianity of an ideal person. Hence it produced no gospel of the life and martyrdom of such a teacher as Aqiba. His disciples might easily have collected his sayings and teaching in a personal form. But it would have been alien to the spirit of Pharisaism for them to do so.'[19]

Christianity differed no less from the ethical systems of the Graeco-Roman world. Socrates, who may be accounted the first moral philosopher, used his famous 'irony' in order to divert

[19] *Judaism and Christianity*, Vol. 1. (London, 1937), pp. 153-4. Abrahams remarked that in Judaism 'the mediate stage between God, the model, and Israel the imitator, consisted mainly of the attributes of God rather than of any concrete exemplifier of those attributes' (*Studies in Pharisaism and the Gospels*, Cambridge 1924, p. 142). It is instructive to note the development of W. D. Davies' thesis in his *Paul and Rabbinic Judaism* (London 1948). In chapter 6 he describes Paul (truly) as one entrusted with a new *torah* based on the words of Jesus; and he suggests (with some plausibility) that apostolic *didache* may have been modelled in part on Jewish codes. But in chapter 7 he argues that, for Paul, it is Jesus himself (as the pre-existent, creative, Wisdom of God) who is the New *Torah* that supersedes the old. The distinctiveness of Jesus' teaching —that which makes it the *new* law of a *new* covenant—is its exemplification in his life.

attention from himself to the truths that he taught. He did not suggest that the Ideas or Forms of moral value were embodied in him or in anyone else. Even Plato, for all his devotion, did not attempt to interpret the master in this light. His metaphysical presuppositions would not have permitted it. The radical contrast that he established between Being and Becoming made an incarnation of absolute values inconceivable.

It is true that in Hellenistic literature the life of Socrates is held up as an example of perfection. The *Encheiridion* of Epictetus tells the reader: 'Even if you are not yet a Socrates, still you ought to live as one who wishes to be a Socrates.' This sentence evokes two comments. Firstly, its sentiment has no basis in the recorded words of Socrates or even in the reflections of Plato, his most profound interpreter. Secondly, in its context it has no more than a pedagogic aim. The fount of Stoic morality is, not an individual example, but the cosmic reason (λόγος) in which all men share. The Stoics never imagined that this λόγος which gave meaning to all that is, could be embodied in an individual human life.[20]

The transition to the Christian fulfilment of moral claims is inevitable. The author of 1 John put it thus. 'In this is love, not that we loved God but that he loved us and sent his Son to be the expiation for our sins. Beloved, if God so loved us, we also ought to love one another' (4. 10-11). The crucial word is 'ought'. Imitation of God is a duty. His sacrificial love imposes on its recipients an obligation to show a like love towards each other.

Similarly Christians are to forgive each other. 'Put on then,' St Paul tells the Colossians, 'compassion, kindness, lowliness, meekness, patience, forbearing one another and, if one has a complaint against another, forgiving each other; as the Lord has forgiven you, so you also must forgive' (3. 12-13). Forgiveness is not a natural virtue, the overflow of a kindly disposition. Like love it is required by the supernatural example of Christ. Like love, too, it takes the form of a response. Christians are morally

---

[20] It has been objected that not even an incarnate God who is also infinite can be imitated by finite beings (See, for example, McTaggart's *Some Dogmas of Religion*, London 1930, pp. 286-88). But we must note two things. The New Testament asks us to imitate only those qualities of Christ that are congruous with our humanity. Secondly it states that we cannot hope to imitate him unless we have his Spirit. This truth was put with special clarity by St Paul in 2 Corinthians 3. 18.

obliged to forgive each other in return for the forgiveness which has been granted to them by God.

The word that best describes this union of imitation and response is 'gratitude'. It is out of gratitude to God that the Christian displays in his conduct the qualities of his Lord. The obligations that Christ's love entails are not the relentless demands of an external law; their constraint is that of favours freely received and freely given. Failure to imitate Christ is not simply failure to follow the highest when we see it; it is not simply treason to our better selves; it is failure in gratitude, an act of disloyalty to the One whom we have known as Saviour and Friend.

Yet we could not imitate Christ and fulfil his claims through our own unaided strength. On account of both original and actual sin we cannot obey God's law unless we receive his free forgiveness and the power of his Spirit. We receive both through Christ who thereby enables us to fulfil his law and share his life.

I cannot here discuss the doctrines of 'grace' and the Holy Spirit in themselves. I can deal only with three questions that arise when we consider their moral implications.

1. It must be admitted that in the New Testament man's incapacity to achieve goodness receives an emphasis that it can never have on the plane of pure morality. The fact of moral failure determines St Paul's whole theology. According to him we can never obtain 'righteousness' by our own efforts to perform the 'works' of the 'law'. We can obtain it only in so far as we are 'justified' (that is, acquitted or forgiven) by God's grace and empowered by his Spirit.

Yet it would be a grave error to suppose that these Pauline statements pervert the 'simple Galilean gospel'. On the contrary they are implied by the whole ministry of Jesus. In particular they are necessitated by the perfectionism of his moral teaching. It is hardly deniable either that his command to love one's enemies is a self-authenticating dictate of the moral law or that its performance is impossible without supernatural aid.[21]

---

[21] At any rate the impracticability of the command was recognized by the eminent Jewish scholar Klausner when he wrote that it is 'too high an ideal for ordinary mankind, and even too high for the man of more than average moral calibre' (*Jesus of Nazareth*, London 1947, pp. 394-5). On the perfectionism of Jesus' moral teaching see Reinhold Niebuhr (*An Interpretation of Christian Ethics*, London 1936 *passim*) and G. F. Thomas (*Christian Ethics and Moral Philosophy*, New York 1955, pp. 32-36).

Revelation deepens the insight that nature itself affords. Even the atheist feels guilt (accompanied by dread) when he recollects his violation of the moral law. Even he can feel the law's inexorable demands. The Gospel illumines both these feeling-states by relating them to God's holy love as their objective cause. Furthermore it offers the only final cure—God's free forgiveness and the power of his Spirit whereby we are enabled to perform his law and imitate his character.

2. It is sometimes said that divine forgiveness imperils the integrity of the moral life by appearing to 'condone' sin. But the New Testament itself answers this criticism by stressing both the cost that God paid for our forgiveness through the sacrifice of Christ and the cost which the sinner too must pay if he is to show the true repentance without which he cannot be forgiven.

The moral structure of forgiveness is pre-eminently simple. God's aim is to make his children good. How is he to achieve his aim? Not by an iron law of retribution (an inflexible cosmic *karma*). This could only lead (as St Paul saw that the Jewish *torah* led) to condemnation. The only course that God can take is to forgive us our sins. And this he has always done. As the Psalmist wrote: 'as far as the east is from the west, so far does he remove our transgressions from us' (103. 12).

Christ did not die in order to make it possible for God to forgive.[22] He died in order to reveal God's love in a form that, by awakening full penitence, enables us to be forgiven. This moral necessity for a divine sacrifice becomes apparent as soon as we consider that the essence of sin is pride—the assertion of our own wills against the known law of God and the known good of our neighbour. Nothing less than the sacrificial love of God can overcome this fatal self-seeking, as St Augustine affirmed in words that penetrate to the moral core of Christian atonement or reconciliation. 'This we do well to believe, nay, to hold fixed and immovable in our hearts, that the humility which God displayed in being born of a woman and in being haled so ignomini-

---

[22] The idea of Christ's death as a substitutionary act that either 'satisfied' God's justice or 'propitiated' his wrath rightly offends the moral sense; but it does not occur in the New Testament which regards the Cross solely as an 'expiation' (a means of annulling guilt and cleansing the sinner by the power of love). On the Biblical evidence see C. H. Dodd's *The Bible and the Greeks* (London 1954, pp. 82-95) and his *Epistle to the Romans* (London 1947, pp. 54-61).

ously by mortal men to death, is the sovereign medicine for healing our swollen pride, the profound mystery (*sacramentum*) by which the bond of sin is broken.'[23]

3. It is sometimes alleged that the idea of supernatural aid, especially when this is described in terms of grace and the Spirit, is incompatible with human freedom. Yet, while certain presentations of these terms have rightly given grounds for this allegation, the Bible unmistakably affirms that human freedom (in the straightforward sense that is presupposed by moral choice) persists throughout the work of divine salvation.

Let us first consider 'grace'. Admittedly if this is taken to mean a mysterious effluence or entity (an ontological *tertium quid*) inhering in and governing the soul it threatens moral freedom. The threat is even more obvious if grace in *any* form is linked with a rigid scheme of individual predestination. But grace in the Pauline (which is the original Christian) sense does not fall into these categories. By χάρις St Paul means the kindness of God in forgiving our sins and restoring us to a right relation with himself through the ministry of Christ.

If, then, we think of grace as the gracious power of God in Christ we cannot consider it to be incompatible with the freedom that the moralist is rightly anxious to conserve. On the contrary it presupposes the believer's free response at every stage. We can always (while still *in via*) choose to reject God's kindness and its transforming power. In so far as grace 'constrains' us it does so wholly by analogy with the good influence exerted by a human person in whose love we trust.

These principles apply no less to the Pauline concept of the Spirit. If the Spirit is conceived as an impersonal and overwhelming force or energy it is bound to imperil freedom. But if, with St Paul, we regard it as God's personal presence in the risen Christ we can see that it, like the grace of which it is a further sign, continually requires a free response. Therefore, St Paul tells the Galatians that though they 'live by' the Spirit they must also 'walk by' the Spirit (that is, behave according to the law of love that the Spirit enjoins).[24] Again, in writing to the Romans he affirms that the Spirit co-operates with believers in order to make them sons of God (8. 14-17).

---

[23] *De trin.* 8. 7. (quoted by J N. D. Kelly in *Early Christian Doctrines*, London 1960, pp. 393-4). [24] Gal. 5. 25-6. 2.

Admittedly there is a paradox (an *apparent* contradiction) in asserting that the Spirit both transforms us by his indwelling power and leaves the freedom of the will intact. The paradox arises (as all religious paradoxes do) because there is no parallel to divine action in the human sphere; for however great may be the influence that finite persons exercise on each other it cannot become an actual indwelling. St Paul could say, 'it is no longer I who live, but Christ who lives in me';[25] but he could not have said this of a merely human person.

It may be possible to make the immanent action of God's grace to some degree intelligible by theological reflection. I myself have tried to do so.[26] But in the end we are confronted with a mystery which is the highest mode of the general mystery inherent in the dependence of the world on God. We cannot *understand* how God both empowers us by his Spirit and preserves our liberty of moral choice. We can only accept—and perhaps experience—it as a fact.[27]

Lastly, revelation fulfils the concept of Beatitude. Reason can suggest that our highest end or goal is to achieve perfection in an everlasting life with God. Yet it is doubtful whether reason alone can convince us that the goal exists.

The New Testament affirms that the goal has already been reached by Christ through his victory over sin and death. Having

[25] Gal. 2. 20.

[26] *Revelation and Existence* (Cardiff 1957, pp. 73-90).

[27] It therefore seems to me that Maclagan seeks for a clarity that is unobtainable when he says that relative to the human will God's action is 'environmental, not constitutive, no matter how intimately environmental it may be' (op. cit. p. 115). His distinction between one's character and one's will is highly abstract (as he himself admits on p. 126). It cannot do justice to spiritual facts. When the Christian says that he has overcome a temptation by God's power he means that God has strengthened his will here and now in the face of contrary desires. Furthermore this simultaneity of divine and human action on the volitional plane is unambiguously affirmed by St Paul in Philippians 2. 12-13. Finally, if Maclagan's own language is to have any clear meaning it must be taken to imply the very view that he rejects. Thus an environmental influence that is sufficiently intimate becomes constitutive; a difference in degree becomes a difference in kind. Again Maclagan concedes that a human will which is in total harmony with the divine is 'energized' by it in a 'frictionless' action (p. 116). I find it very hard to conceive a spiritual energizing without a spiritual contact.

offered a perfect sacrifice he is now exalted 'at the right hand of the Father'.[28] He did not merely discourse about beatitude; he actually achieved it by his obedience to the Father's will.

God promises believers that, through the Spirit, they can share in the beatitude won for them by Christ who is 'the first-born among many brethren', the inclusive head of a 'new creation'. Thus St Paul writes in the chapter of Romans to which I have already referred: 'When we cry, "Abba! Father!" it is the Spirit himself bearing witness with our spirit that we are children of God, and if children, then heirs, heirs of God and fellow heirs with Christ, provided we suffer with him in order that we may also be glorified with him' (8. 15-17).

The concluding words are the morally crucial ones: 'provided we suffer with him in order that we may be glorified with him'. Christians cannot share the glory of their Lord unless they share his death—unless they are crucified with him to their lower selves and to the vanity of this fleeting world. This spiritual law whereby we gain life through death was stated by the Lord himself. 'If any man would come after me, let him deny himself and take up his cross daily and follow me. For whoever would save his life will lose it; and whoever loses his life for my sake, he will save it.'[29]

Yet the way of sacrifice is more than the condition of an immortality that is yet to come. It is itself the beginning of eternal life. 'We know that we *have passed* out of death into life, because we love the brethren.'[30] In a real (though hidden) way each act of love (or of any other virtue when controlled by love) joins us to Christ in the eternal world where he for ever reigns as our Example and High-Priest.

The Christian lives simultaneously both in 'this age' which is doomed to pass away and to 'the coming age' which has been brought within his reach by Christ. His task is to embody (as far as possible) the life of the new age within the context of the old. This is the ever-present moral meaning of his daily prayer: 'Thy Kingdom come.'

[28] See the *Epistle to the Hebrews* (passim).

[29] Lk. 9.23. The paradox that Jesus here propounds is a final answer to those who hold that the hope of beatitude is inimical to morality. Only those who love the good for its own sake (or rather for the sake of its Exemplar) can obtain the eternal life that they rightly seek.

[30] 1 Jn. 3. 14.

In this earthly life God's Reign will never *fully* come. The Christian is constantly afflicted by evil in both its moral and non-moral forms. Yet he has ground for endless hope. Because of the victory won for him by Christ he knows that no aspiration after goodness and no enactment of it can be lost. In so far as they are inspired by Christ they already belong to the eternal order that will be unveiled at his Parousia.

A. E. Taylor summed up this eschatological transformation of morality in words on which it would be scarcely possible to improve : —

'Now if the central doctrine of the Christian is true, then we have such a certainty as the world cannot otherwise afford that love and duty are indeed sacred. For then it is a fact that the Master of all things has not merely told us to be loving and dutiful and will hold us to account if we fail; He has Himself, in the person of the historical Lord Jesus, entered into the life of humanity, has Himself led the life of selfless love and duty to the bitter end, and triumphed over all the obstacles that beset it; we, who have still the obstacles and hindrances to conflict with, have received from him not merely the inspiration of His teaching and example, but the certainty that the values which are sustained by the eternal "living will" are precisely those which were affirmed in practice by the Lord Jesus and are dearest to our own hearts— love, dutifulness, humility, courage, patience. We know, then, that, however appearances may be against them, these values can "never fail"; they are the foundation-stones on which the frame of things is built.'[31]

There is one other argument on which I ought to touch. It is sometimes said that the truth of Christian theism is authenticated by the moral excellence of Christian lives. Thus, for example, Charles Gore wrote : —

'I do not hesitate to say that one of the deepest reasons for believing that Christianity must be true is the evidence of the lives of those who throughout the centuries have shown themselves to be real and whole-hearted Christians. This is a never-ceasing evidence which appeals to us all. We cannot but believe

[31] *The Christian Hope of Immortality* (London 1946, pp. 61-2).

that a creed which can produce such a result, on such a scale, and over such a length of ages, must be in some deep correspondence with reality.'[32]

Yet this argument, even when supported by impressive evidence, is exposed to two objections. Firstly, is not conspicuous virtue often found among those who adhere to non-Christian systems of religion or philosophy? But is not the Christian obliged to say that these systems are untrue? Secondly, I have admitted that atheists often equal, if not excel, Christians in performing works of love. How then can these works prove supernatural activity?

I do not believe that the first objection is insuperable. We oversimplify a complex matter if we say that non-Christian systems of religion and philosophy are false. They all contain *some* truth, even if in a distorted form; and the truth could account for those moral qualities that we admire in their adherents. Thus, while the Christian cannot endorse the Hindu concept of Brahman, he can regard it as an attempt to express the truth that absolute Being transcends finite particularity. He can then hold that the detachment and compassion which the Hindu sage achieves is due to a genuine (though clouded) grasp of ultimate reality.

The second objection carries much greater weight. I doubt whether it can be answered satisfactorily. I do not believe that the truth-claims of Christianity can be *conclusively* verified by an appeal to Christian lives. Even if we had evidence that Christian goodness is superior to any goodness which an atheist can achieve we should still not be obliged to conclude that Christian belief is true. The most we need say is that it is effective. We could not infer 'true' from 'effective' by appealing again to Christian lives. Nor could we infer it by applying an *a priori* principle.[33]

However, Christian goodness provides *confirmatory* evidence.

---

[32] *The Philosophy of the Good Life* (London 1946, p. 282).

[33] Some apologists attempt to argue from moral effects to a divine cause by claiming, more generally, that Christian faith 'integrates' and 'gives significance' to life. But once again we cannot infer 'true' from 'effective' without committing a *petitio principii*. Furthermore, Christians sometimes feel, and perhaps appear, disintegrated and (so far as this world is concerned) despairing. They certainly live in hope of achieving peace through God; but to the unbeliever the hope is bound to seem illusory.

In this it is on a par with miracles (as is indicated by the fact that we sometimes call it a 'miracle' of grace). Just as we cannot prove Christ's divinity by a formal deduction from his miracles (for there were other miracle-workers in the ancient world), so we cannot prove divine causality from goodness (for the same, or very similar, goodness is discoverable in unbelievers). But just as we can take Christ's miracles as secondary signs of a divinity that is primarily revealed in other ways, so we can take the goodness of the saint—and even our own lesser moral victories—as secondary evidence for the divine Goodness who is primarily known to us on other grounds.

There are two viewpoints from which this supernatural evidence for faith can be surveyed.

Firstly, the evidence is historical. It consists in both the teaching of Jesus himself and the significance which his ministry acquired in apostolic thought. It seems to me clear that the second strand in this evidence is insecure unless it is based on the first. We could not reasonably believe that Jesus was the incarnation of God's love unless we had substantial grounds for this belief in his recorded words and acts.

Secondly, we have the fact that Christianity fulfils the knowledge of God that is obtainable through rational reflection on the moral order. While the idea of an infinitely good Creator stems from revelation, reason can discern that his existence is demanded by the moral consciousness. This train of reasoning is in turn confirmed and amplified by the ministry of Christ.

Clearly it is invalid to argue for the truth of Christianity *solely* on the ground that it fulfils the theistic implications of morality. A 'mythical' Christ (that is, a Christ who is merely a symbol of God-Manhood, as various Gnostics, Hegelians and Existentialists have considered him to be) could not be the satisfaction of our moral needs. Only a real incarnation for which there is sufficient evidence can support my argument. That the evidence is sufficient I wholeheartedly believe; but the proof of its sufficiency falls outside the limits of this book.

However, there is an intermediate attitude which merits our attention. Let us suppose that someone is convinced that Christ claimed a unique authority, that he practised (as well as taught) universal love, that those who knew him best saw in his death

the sacrificial love of God, and that he fulfilled the highest in-
tuitions of the Old Testament. Let us suppose too that the same
person finds it hard to endorse the message of the New Testament with the full, personal, assent of faith. Surely he would be
helped towards belief if he came to see that Christ fulfils, not
only the Old Testament, but also the deepest requirements of
his own moral life.

It is at any rate remarkable (and as sure a sign of Providence
as any known to me) that the rational and *a priori* implications
of morality coincide so perfectly with fact (or rather, let us say,
with the facts as they are described in the New Testament). The
facts belong to history. The minds of those who recorded them
were unphilosophical. Yet the facts and their interpretation
illumine and embody the theistic bearings of those moral principles that philosophy investigates.

However, the appeal to facts and their congruity with our
natural understanding of the moral order must be completed by
a reference to the role that is occupied by the Church. Christian
belief arose, and continues, within the divine community. I do
not say that a person cannot be converted, or even persevere in
faith, outside the visible Church. He may well do so. But even
then it is through the Church (and, more widely, through the
life of Christendom) that the Gospel has reached him in his
secular existence. And it is *normally* in the Church that the
Christian learns the *full* meaning of the law of Christ.

This leads me to say a word on the question of 'authority'.
In a general, and important, sense religion always depends to
some extent on the authority of those who have enjoyed a
special form or degree of insight into 'things divine'. Within
Christianity in particular our knowledge of God is derived from
the experience of inspired men firstly in the apostolic age and
secondly in the later ages of the Church.

Most of us, in speaking of the moral transformation which is
available through Christ, do not mean that we have experienced
it with the fulness that was granted to St Francis or St Paul. We
owe to them—and to many others known and unknown—the
lesser experience that is ours. We also owe to them the confirmation of our hope that we, who share with them God's grace,
will also share with them the perfection that his grace confers.

This, then, concludes my survey of the moral evidence for Christian theism. My arguments are neither necessary nor sufficient for belief in God. They are not necessary, for the simplest mind can grasp God pre-philosophically through the natural law and Christian revelation. They are not sufficient, for (as I have often stressed) discursive reason must give way to intuition if we are to obtain the certitude of faith. *Non in dialectica complacuit Deo salvum facere populum suum.*

Yet even dialectic has its part to play. It can precede faith and awaken it. It can also succeed faith and confirm it. How far my presentation of the moral argument can help to awaken faith I would not dare to say. It is too much to hope that my reasoning is uniformly cogent. But at least I hope that some of the evidence I have given is sufficient to persuade an inquiring mind that only Christian theism explains and unifies the moral life.

I fully realize that speculative reasoning is often disparaged or ignored by contemporary philosophers and theologians. But I am convinced that this disparagement is a passing fashion. The non-rational routes to God that Existentialists propose may have the fascination of apparent novelty; but they cannot sustain us to the end; for it is in the eternal Logos who was made Man in Christ that we by nature live and move and have our being.

INDEX OF NAMES

DATE DUE

OCT 41 71

DEC 22 75

DEC 2 1978

NOV 75

MAY 1992

JAN 27 1992

FEB 1 1992

JUN 01 2002

PRINTED IN U.S.A.

GAYLORD